RESCUE

DARING MISSIONS FROM ON, UNDER AND ABOVE THE EARTH

DAVID LONG

Illustrated by Kerry Hyndman

FABER & FABER

In Memory of Andrew Patrick Veal (1961–2018) – DL

For Sylvia G, with love – KH

This edition first published in the UK in 2019
This edition first published in the USA in 2020
by Faber and Faber Limited
Bloomsbury House
74–77 Great Russell Street
London WC1B 3DA
This paperback edition first published in 2020

Designed by Faber and Faber
Printed in India

978-0-571-34633-2

2 4 6 8 10 9 7 5 3 1

CONTENTS

When disasters strike, we are all grateful to the rescue services whose job it is to swoop in and save the day. It's easy to forget that these organisations are made up of individual people, who may be trained experts, but nonetheless risk their own lives each time they go to work. Perhaps even more astonishing are the ordinary men, women and children who find themselves caught up in other people's dramas and, instead of running away, do everything they can to help.

Whether dragging a friend from a blazing car, leading a search far below the earth's surface or rescuing astronauts from a space mission that went badly wrong, the extraordinary stories in this book reveal the ingenuity, courage and determination of the human spirit. All of the stories are true, the people involved come from all over the world and their exploits are amazing, eye-opening and truly inspiring.

John McCants and Bill Lowrey
A daring mid-air rescue
(USA, 1941)

One morning in May 1941, Walter Osipoff was getting ready to jump out of an aeroplane. It was flying more than a thousand metres above the ground, but as an experienced parachutist in the US Marines he'd made many such jumps before. There was nothing about this one that made him think it would be any different.

This particular jump involved a dozen soldiers and some large canisters full of rifles and other military equipment. The heavy canisters were fitted with their own parachutes, and one of them had

He'd done this before too, but this time something went badly wrong

already been pushed out through the hatch of the Douglas DC-2. Walter steadied himself to eject the second one and was planning to jump after it.

He'd done this before too, but this time something went badly wrong. The rip cord that was meant to open his parachute after he jumped had somehow become tangled up with another rip cord attached to the canister. This caused the two parachutes to open too soon, while they were still inside the aircraft. Both started billowing like sails on a yacht, and Walter and the canister were immediately sucked out of the aircraft by the wind rushing past the hatch. A second or two later he found himself dangling beneath the tail of the plane, where he quickly became tangled up in a huge knot of cord, cables and parachute fabric.

The first that pilot Harold Johnson knew of this was when the pull of the two parachutes caused the nose of the DC-2 to tilt dangerously upwards. Wrestling with the controls, he managed to get the aircraft back into position, and shortly afterwards realised what had gone wrong. The aircraft's crew were trying desperately to haul Walter back inside, but this proved impossible. All Harold could do now was fly around in circles while someone back at base came up with a plan.

Down on the ground several other soldiers and airmen could see something dangling from the plane, although it took them a while to realise it was a man and not a piece of equipment. Walter had been badly injured in the incident, catching his arm and shoulder on a jagged piece of metal as he was pulled out of the aircraft. Four of the taut parachute lines were now biting into his face and body, and he was in real danger of smashing into the fuselage.

He didn't know it but the DC-2 was also running out of fuel. Harold could see this from his instruments, but he couldn't land until Walter had been pulled back inside, or been somehow untangled from the lines.

Watching from the ground was another pilot, Lieutenant Bill Lowrey. He yelled at his colleagues to put some fuel into a Curtiss Seagull biplane and grabbed a sharp knife from a nearby marine. Without waiting for permission, he and fellow pilot John McCants took to the sky. Before long they had their biplane in position beneath Walter's wildly swinging body, but they couldn't get close enough to catch him. If they flew too close the little Seagull got buffeted around by the other, much larger plane.

With barely ten minutes' fuel left in the DC-2, Harold climbed to a higher altitude in the hope that this would reduce the air turbulence. This seemed to work and the Seagull followed him up there.

Bill fought to keep the biplane steady. He knew he had to keep the Seagull's spinning propeller away from the injured parachutist and ensure that its blades didn't tangle with the two parachutes. If this happened one or both aircraft would almost certainly crash. The Seagull and DC-2 were travelling at more than a hundred miles an hour, hundreds of metres up in the air.

Bill fought to keep the biplane steady

Now, in a truly death-defying manoeuvre, John managed to stand up and reach out to Walter. It took at least five attempts, but eventually John was

able to grab hold of him. Pulling the soldier's head down into his section of the cockpit, he struggled to get Walter's body down on to the top of the fuselage.

Walter could fall off at any moment, and he was still attached to the other aircraft by the cords of the parachutes. Everyone knew that the two aircraft wouldn't be able to hold this close position for very long. While Bill concentrated on flying as close as he dared to the DC-2, John grabbed the marine's knife. Using one hand to stop Walter falling off the Seagull, he used the other to saw away at the tough nylon lines which effectively tied all three of them to the DC-2.

It seemed to take forever, but they were all now at a point of no return. If John couldn't cut Walter free, or if the plane ran out of fuel, they would all perish together.

As vital seconds ticked away, disaster struck again: the Seagull's propeller hit the end of the DC-2. A foot-long section of its tail fell away, but to Bill's surprise and relief, both aircraft were still in the air. At the same time the propeller also sliced through the tangle of lines and cables which John had been frantically attacking with the knife. This meant the DC-2 could at last fly off and land before its fuel tanks ran dry.

As vital seconds ticked away, disaster struck again

Five of the men were now safe, but the same couldn't be said for the three in the little Seagull. Bill and John didn't know yet whether Walter's injuries were even survivable, but they all found themselves facing another deadly hazard.

Almost as soon as it was cut free by the propeller, one of the parachutes had become caught up again. This time it was jammed into the part of the biplane's tail, which acts as a rudder. This meant the Seagull couldn't steer properly, but nobody could do anything to help. John was clinging to Walter to prevent him falling to his death, and Bill obviously couldn't leave the plane's controls.

The men could only hope that luck was on their side – and, finally, this time, it was. With incredible skill the Seagull's pilot managed to bring his plane down in one piece. After thirty-three minutes of being dragged behind the DC-2, where he was bounced around like a ping-pong ball in a storm, Walter Osipoff looked like he was safe.

He was unconscious by the time he was taken to hospital, but happily he survived and his injuries healed. Six months later he was back in the air, wearing another parachute and getting ready for another jump. Almost as remarkable, John and Bill had gone back to work that same afternoon as if nothing had happened.

Six months later he was back in the air

Three weeks later the pair were awarded the Distinguished Flying Cross for their extraordinary courage and skill in performing what is still regarded as one of the most dangerous and amazing rescues in American aviation history.

LIN HAO
A schoolboy's duty to his classmates (China, 2008)

On 12 May 2008 a powerful earthquake struck Sichuan in China, killing more than 70,000 men, women and children. The people of this beautiful mountainous region had experienced many earthquakes before, but this was easily the worst for as long as anyone could remember. It caused billions of pounds worth of damage to homes, offices and factories, and is now known to have been the third most powerful earthquake ever recorded anywhere in the world.

Over a thousand miles away in Shanghai many buildings shook and people could see modern tower blocks actually swaying from side to side. In Sichuan itself more than five million people were made homeless, and in addition to the horrifying death toll a staggering 375,000 others needed medical treatment for their injuries. Thousands more were reported missing, and as far away as Pakistan the tremors could still be felt more than ten minutes later.

Nine-year-old Lin Hao was at school in YingXui when disaster struck. The town was at the epicentre of the earthquake, meaning the place where its destructive power was greatest. People living in YingXui were more badly affected than anywhere else, and in less than two minutes their town was almost completely demolished. Four out of every five buildings were left in ruins, and bridges collapsed, crushing cars and trucks like they were toys. Moments later, boulders bigger than apartment blocks tumbled down from the nearby mountains, causing even more destruction.

In less than two minutes their town was almost completely demolished

One of the largest buildings in YingXui was the Middle School. It had been built of modern, reinforced concrete only two years earlier, but it too collapsed in seconds. With no time to escape, several hundred children were killed, buried under tonnes of concrete and steel. Little Lin Hao was too young to be a pupil there, but his own much smaller school was similarly affected.

When he first felt the tremors he was walking along a corridor with two of his classmates. As their world shook and the walls and ceiling caved in, Lin Hao and his friends were probably too confused to realise what was going on. Seconds later the two friends were lying unconscious in the rubble, and Lin Hao was struggling to breathe and looking for a way out

Lin Hao's head was hurting. He knew he had been hit by something, but he was lucky that nothing too heavy had fallen on him. Other children in the school had been knocked unconscious by falling masonry or pinned down by large pieces of wall or ceiling so that they couldn't move. Lin Hao found he could move, and began struggling to climb out of the terrifying mess. He'd never experienced an earthquake before, but something told him he had to get out of the building as fast as possible.

He had to get out of the building as fast as possible

Once he was outside he could see that his school had been almost totally destroyed in those first few seconds. He then did a truly remarkable thing. Having escaped from the wreckage, and despite having an injury to his head, he turned around and went straight back into the ruined school. He couldn't see his two friends anywhere, and he didn't know yet whether they were alive or dead. All he knew was that if they were still inside the building he had to try to get them out.

Whenever there is news of a huge natural disaster or fire on television we get used to the sight of people running away. It's such a natural response to flee from danger that it's easy to forget how much courage it must take for rescue workers to run towards the danger. Police and fire-fighters do this all the time, deliberately putting themselves at risk when everyone else is running in the opposite direction. It's what these men and women do for a living, it's what they are paid for, but it is still incredibly brave.

Nobody would expect a young child to do the same thing, but that's exactly what Lin Hao did.

Without stopping to think about the risk he was taking, or worrying about the pain in his head, he went back into the building and began looking for his two friends. Even after an ordinary earthquake this is an extremely dangerous thing to do, but after a big one it is many times worse. Tremors called aftershocks carry on long after the first wave of destruction. This means that even if a building appears to have survived the earthquake it can suddenly collapse after one of these later tremors.

Lin Hao didn't seem worried about any of this. He had only one thing on his mind, which was to get his friends out alive. Crawling on his hands and knees, he had to take great care to avoid shards of broken glass and other pieces of debris that were scattered all over what had been the floor of the school. This meant the little boy had to go slowly, so it took a while to get back to the spot where he and his friends had been walking when the disaster struck.

He had only one thing on his mind, which was to get his friends out alive

Once he got there, it didn't take Lin Hao long to find the first of his classmates. Still on his hands and knees, he managed to pull him out of the wreckage before crawling back in a second time to look for the other one. His other friend took slightly longer to find. He was still unconscious, but Lin Hao somehow managed to carry him out of danger.

Sadly, many of their classmates were not so lucky, and more than twenty children were killed in the initial collapse. With so much terrible news from the earthquake, people were desperate to hear something positive and uplifting. The story of Lin Hao's extraordinary heroism gave them hope,

and it was soon being reported on television programmes and in newspapers around the world.

Three months later the little boy was asked to carry the Chinese flag around the arena at the Beijing Olympics. This was a great honour for Lin Hao, and almost everybody he met there congratulated him on being such a hero. He knew he'd done something special, but refused to be big-headed about it. Instead he told people, 'I was the hall monitor, it was my job to look after my classmates.'

MIKE HAILWOOD

Braving the flames to save a friend (South Africa, 1973)

Britain's 'Mike the Bike' was a famous and hugely popular world champion motorcycle rider. The fans loved him and were thrilled when he won the famous Isle of Man TT race no fewer than twelve times. He also won nine world championships, so there was great excitement when he announced he was switching from two wheels to four and planned to have a go at competing in Formula One.

Racing these single-seaters used to be even more dangerous than it is now. When the sport first began Formula One cars weren't fitted with any safety equipment at all, and grand prix drivers were not even required to wear a seatbelt. More than fifty top drivers were killed driving at speeds of up to 200 miles an hour, and for many years it was rare for a racing season to finish without at least one death along the way.

In the 1970s, when Mike Hailwood began racing cars at this level, terrible accidents happened often. The decade was one of the deadliest in motorsport's long history. Nine drivers lost their lives in the Formula One championship, and many more were killed in other types of races. The circuits were often much longer than modern ones, which meant that emergency teams were rarely anywhere near the scene of a crash. Also, the races took place in all weathers, including heavy rain. When this happened, car brakes and tyres didn't work very well on the wet surface, and the resulting spray made it much harder for drivers to see where they were going.

Mike was involved in one of these high-speed accidents in March 1973. It happened during the South African Grand Prix at the Kyalami Circuit. On only the third lap, and with no warning, his powerful Surtees-Ford was suddenly hit by a Lotus and then again by another car belonging to a Swiss driver called Clay Regazzoni. Mike's car was badly damaged: fuel spilled out of its split tank on to the track and caught fire. Out of the race, but apparently uninjured, he clambered free of the wreckage and immediately tried to rescue his rival.

Clay had been knocked unconscious by the force of the collision, and his BRM car had also burst into flames. Mike raced over to it, ignoring the obvious dangers. With no fear for his own safety, he began trying to undo the injured driver's harness so that he could lift him out of the cockpit. It was a struggle and, after only a few seconds, the heat of the flames had become so unbearable he had to back off.

As Mike staggered away from the blaze, anxious spectators could see that his racing boots and fuel-soaked overalls had already caught fire. Film of the incident shows Mike frantically waving his burning arms around and shouting to a trackside safety marshal who had just arrived with a fire extinguisher.

His racing boots and fuel-soaked overalls had already caught fire

A single fire extinguisher wasn't going to be enough to save Clay or his car, but the marshal was able to tackle the flames that were licking around Mike's hands, feet and face. As soon as these had been put out, and to the astonishment of the watching crowd, Mike immediately had another attempt at pulling the unconscious Clay out of his car.

Everyone could see that the BRM was almost totally engulfed in a ferocious inferno: it was burning out of control. Mike nevertheless dived straight into the fire and smoke, determined to have second go at getting his friend out before it was too late.

This time, amazingly, he managed to do it, loosening the harness and pulling the driver free. After being carried to safety, the still unconscious Clay was rushed to hospital. Mike meanwhile walked back to the team workshop, located in an area to one side of the track known as the pits.

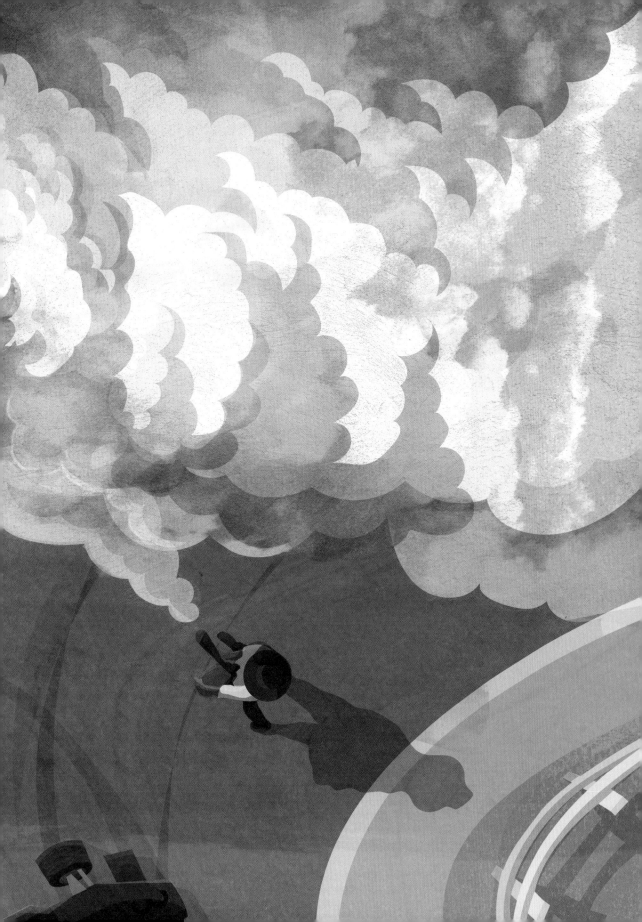

It says a lot about the Englishman's quiet modesty that when he got back to the pits he didn't say anything to anyone about what he had just done. Instead he and his girlfriend Pauline left the circuit for the day and went back to their hotel. It was only the following morning, when Pauline read the newspaper headlines, that she realised that Mike had done something incredibly courageous.

When Clay regained consciousness, and despite the ferocity of the blaze, he seemed to have suffered only minor burns. From the state of his burned-out car it was obvious that he had been incredibly lucky to have escaped with such light injuries. It was also clear that it was Mike's sudden, selfless and instinctive act of heroism which had saved his friend's life.

Clay made a rapid recovery and he was soon back racing again. Mike was also back in action the following month when he took part in the Spanish Grand Prix at the wheel of another Surtees car. He didn't win the race, but at the end of the year his heroism was officially recognised when he was awarded the George Medal. This is Britain's second highest civilian award for bravery.

It was Mike's sudden selfless and instinctive act of heroism which had saved his friend's life

Mike carried on racing for another year but was never able to achieve the same success in Formula One that he had enjoyed on two wheels. Despite this, his heroic actions in South Africa meant that he was more popular than ever with spectators, and this made it even more shocking when he was killed a few years later in a tragic road accident.

Mike was taking his children to collect some fish and chips when his car was involved in a collision. A truck driver made an illegal turn. Mike's nine-year-old daughter was killed almost immediately, and Mike the Bike died a couple of days later from his injuries.

His six-year-old son somehow survived the crash, but Mike's death on an ordinary, quiet road sent shockwaves through the close-knit motorsports community. At his funeral his coffin was carried into the church by friends, including drivers, riders and another three world champions. A few years later, in a strange and horrible echo of the tragedy, another freak road accident claimed the life of Clay Regazzoni. Once again it was a collision involving a truck.

JESSICA MCCLURE
The girl who fell down a well
(USA, 1987)

Sometimes the most ordinary places can turn out to be the most dangerous ones. When little Jessica McClure was playing with friends in her aunt's garden one Wednesday morning, no one expected the toddler to slip and fall down an old, disused well.

The well was deep but extremely narrow, and for a while it was impossible to know if the eighteen-month-old girl had survived the fall. In fact, Jessica had become trapped about seven metres below the surface, but when she first disappeared her parents, Chip and Cissy, couldn't hear or see anything down in the dark shaft.

The emergency services were called and help arrived almost immediately. Neighbours, family, police and fire crews all crowded into the garden in the Texas town of Midland, desperately hoping the little girl was all right. A special microphone on a long lead was slowly lowered into the mouth of the well, and the people standing around were told to keep quiet.

Everyone strained to hear a sound, any sound, from deep underground. At first there was nothing, and Chip and Cissy began to fear the worst. It was only when the microphone at last picked up a tiny, frightened voice that they knew Jessica was alive. Even then no one knew how – or even if – it would be possible to get her out of the deep well.

The well shaft was only about twenty centimetres wide and luckily it was no longer full of water. A small video camera was lowered down after the microphone, and the pictures showed that Jessica was firmly wedged in a slight bend in the shaft. She was only a few metres from safety, but the shaft was too narrow for anyone to reach her or to go down and lift her out.

The obvious solution seemed to be to make the hole bigger, but this was quickly ruled out as a possibility. The well was surrounded by solid rock. Digging it out would take too long. Time was a crucial factor, because Jessica wouldn't be able to survive for long without food or water. But if the rescue team used heavy machinery to do the work more quickly, she would be at great risk from falling rocks.

As the day wore on there was still no sign of a firm rescue plan. Television crews and reporters began arriving in Midland to cover the story. As darkness fell powerful floodlights were switched on around the well, and by the following morning millions of Americans were watching the scene and waiting nervously for some news. Everyone wanted to see the little girl emerge from the hole, happy and smiling – but nobody in the garden seemed to know quite what to do.

Much of the area around this part of West Texas is mining country, and at the time of Jessica's accident many people in Midland had jobs in the oil industry. Extracting oil from underground involves drilling large, deep holes called oil wells. This meant there were lots of professional mining engineers living and working locally. Several of them raced into Midland in the hope they could help the police and fire departments devise a way to rescue Jessica McClure.

Even with so many experts on hand it took a while to work out the best course of action. Eventually it was decided to drill a second shaft alongside the well, and then to dig a tunnel from one shaft to the other. If the second shaft was made wider than the well, it would be possible for someone to go down it and then bring Jessica along the tunnel and back up to the surface.

It was important to avoid drilling too close to the well or Jessica would still be in danger

The idea sounded like it might work, but it was very risky. Even with the best equipment the oil industry could supply, it would still take many hours to penetrate the solid rock. A machine known as a rat-hole rig could do the work, but it was important to avoid drilling too close to the well or Jessica would still be in danger from any dislodged falling rocks. This meant the connecting tunnel would have to be longer (and take longer to dig), but no one could think of a better way to rescue her.

Oxygen was piped down the well to help Jessica breathe, and on the second day members of the rescue team could hear her singing softly into the microphone. The song they heard was one of her favourites, from *Winnie the Pooh*. This was really good news. It showed she was still conscious, although it wasn't possible to tell if she was injured, and if so how badly.

As the noisy drilling machines began work, Jessica's mother spent the time singing along with her daughter. Cissy hoped that hearing these familiar nursery rhymes would take Jessica's mind off how cold and hungry she was, and how long she had been trapped down the hole. Sometimes Jessica sounded quite happy, but at other times she cried out for her mother. After nearly two days and a night underground she was becoming dangerously dehydrated and must have been terribly lonely.

As time ticked away, Jessica cried more and more, only stopping when she fell asleep for a while. Although the sleep would do her good, the silence was more disturbing for everyone waiting on the surface. At least when Jessica was crying or singing, they knew she was still alive.

At least when Jessica was crying or singing, they knew she was still alive

The situation was becoming more and more desperate. Without being able to eat or drink, Jessica was growing weaker. Her parents were also worried that if she lost even a small amount of weight it would increase the danger of her slipping further down the well. If that happened it would be impossible to get her out.

The plight of the poor trapped girl was now headline news. Around the world, churches were holding vigils for Jessica. Millions of strangers were praying for her safe recovery, but as night fell at the end of the second day the police were still unable to say how long it might take to bring her out.

After a team of mining engineers had spent all night drilling it was decided that the second shaft was deep enough. Now, ten metres down, the really hard work could begin and miners began digging out a tunnel by hand to connect the shaft to the well. This was done by a team of men taking turns down the hole. Each one had to lie flat on his stomach and use a powered chisel known as a jackhammer to cut through the solid rock.

This part of the operation was guided by a government mining expert who had flown to Texas to help. He said the tunnel must be angled so that it entered the well below the place where Jessica was stuck. This would prevent any debris dropping on to her, and avoid the very real risk of her becoming dislodged as the men broke through the wall of the well. Everything possible had to be done to minimise the danger of the child falling further down the shaft.

The work was tough and exhausting, even for men used to digging underground

The work was tough and exhausting, even for men used to digging underground. The second shaft was only seventy-six centimetres wide, and conditions at the bottom were cramped and uncomfortable. In the dark and sweltering heat, the diggers had to work as fast as possible – but also extremely carefully. Any sudden movement or vibration from the heavy jackhammers could cause the sides of the well to fall in on Jessica.

It took until Friday for the hard-working tunnellers to break through to the well, and it was getting dark again by the time the hole was large enough to reach Jessica. Getting this far had taken a massive team effort and more than fifty-eight hours. Now the final stage of the rescue fell to a specialist paramedic, Robert O'Donnell. Under the floodlights' glare he inched his way slowly through the narrow opening before carefully lifting the exhausted child to safety.

Jessica had been alone in the dark for three days and two nights, an ordeal that for a while made her the most famous baby in the world. She had cuts and bruises from the fall, and would need an operation to amputate a badly damaged toe. She'd also lost nearly a fifth of her bodyweight and was dangerously

> Jessica had been alone in the dark for three days and two nights

dehydrated. Fortunately she went on to make a full recovery, and now lives a normal life with two children of her own, in a house just a couple of miles away from the well that nearly killed her.

SS *Andrea Doria*
Disaster in the fog
(Atlantic Ocean, 1956)

When Piero Calamai set sail for New York he did so as captain of Italy's largest, fastest and most luxurious ocean liner. More than 212 metres in length, the SS *Andrea Doria* had room on board for nearly 1,250 passengers and 600 crew. Many people at the time thought she was the most beautiful ship anywhere in the world.

On deck there were three different swimming pools, and the walls of the restaurants, bars and ballroom were decorated with more than a million dollars' worth of spectacular art. What passengers nicknamed the *Doria* was also technologically highly advanced for the time. Her hull was constructed using two layers of thick steel and divided into eleven watertight compartments. According to the designer and the ship's builders, two of these compartments could fill completely with seawater and the *Doria* still wouldn't sink.

Unusually, the liner also had two separate radar systems, which the captain and crew could use to locate any ships nearby that might otherwise pose a danger.

Enormously popular with businessmen and tourists alike, and a source of great national pride for many Italians, the *Doria* had successfully completed a hundred Atlantic crossings before Captain Calamai set off on the fateful 101st. The journey from Genoa in Italy to the United States usually took nine days and for much of the time, crossing more than 3,000 miles of vast, empty ocean, it was rare even to see another ship. But by the ninth day the *Doria* had arrived in more crowded waters off the coast of Nantucket. As darkness began to fall the passengers and crew knew they were nearing their destination.

There was a thick fog that night, but Captain Calamai was keen to reach New York on time. The *Doria* was steaming ahead at almost full speed when she was struck hard, at around 11 p.m., by the MS *Stockholm*. This was Sweden's largest passenger ship, which was by chance travelling in the opposite direction back to Europe. She too was equipped

There was a thick fog that night, but Captain Calamai was keen to reach New York on time with radar, but unfortunately, by the time any of the sailors on either vessel had spotted the other one, it was too late for either of them to slow down or to change course to avoid a collision.

Five Swedish sailors were killed immediately as one lumbering steel giant piled into the other. The bow of their ship was smashed and torn off, the whole front section of the hull crumpling as if it had been made of cardboard or plastic. The *Stockholm* remained afloat, somehow, but the *Doria* didn't stand a chance.

Several sailors and passengers had been killed on the *Doria* too, and a fourteen-year-old girl, who was knocked out of bed by the force of the collision, woke up to find she had been thrown on to the other ship. Incredibly, Linda Morgan survived this ordeal (unlike her father and little sister), but within moments the *Doria* was leaning perilously over to one side. Five enormous fuel tanks had been ripped open, and hundreds of tonnes of icy seawater poured in through a huge gash in the steel hull.

The crews of both ships sprang into action straight away. Realising that his own vessel was certain to sink, Captain Calamai gave the order to abandon ship. Unfortunately, because the *Doria* was leaning so heavily, at least eight lifeboats on one side could not be launched. Without these the captain could not see how it would be possible to get the 1,700 men, women and children off the ship safely. He asked for a desperate SOS message to be sent using the ship's radio: *Danger immediate. Need lifeboats – as many as possible.*

Danger immediate. Need lifeboats – as many as possible

This was the worst collision in American waters for more than forty years, but in a way it was lucky that it happened where it did. There were many other ships travelling across this part of the Atlantic. As soon as the radio message was heard by the crews of those sailing nearby, several captains quickly changed course to help the stricken liner.

The crew of the *Stockholm* meanwhile began rescuing as many people as they could see through the fog and darkness. Other passengers tried to clamber on to a small cargo vessel, which was the first to arrive on the scene. It was quickly followed by a US Navy warship and a troop carrier.

Already dangerous, the situation on the *Doria* was worsening as the minutes passed. Italy's pride and joy was still just about afloat, but several passengers had plunged into the sea after slipping down her wooden decks, which were now wet and steeply angled.

Some passengers were trapped in their cabins by falling debris

Next to join the rescue was another huge liner, a French ship called the *Ile de France*. This had travelled from more than forty miles away and by around two o'clock in the morning her captain had managed to manoeuvre alongside the ruined *Doria* so that some of those still left on board could scramble to safety.

Not everyone was able to do this. Some passengers were trapped in their cabins by falling debris, or on stairways and in corridors that had become blocked or flooded. Other parts of the ship were filling up with choking black smoke from the engines.

With the *Doria* likely to sink at any moment, nothing could be done to save many of these passengers, especially those who were stuck on the lower decks. Tragically, forty-six passengers and crew died in this way, and at around 5.30 a.m. Captain Calamai boarded the last lifeboat, knowing that

everyone who could be taken off safely had been. By this time more than 750 people were crowded on to the already packed French liner. Another 545 had joined the shocked passengers on the *Stockholm*, and 365 had been rescued by the freighter's crew and by sailors of the US Navy.

Unsurprisingly, some were injured or bruised, many were cold and wet, and everyone was uncomfortable in the cramped conditions – but they were safe and they were alive. A total of 1,660 people had been saved from the wreck of the *Doria*, which was even more than went down in the *Titanic*. This makes it one of the largest rescues in maritime history.

Amazingly one person managed to sleep through the entire incident

Amazingly, one person managed to sleep through the entire incident. Robert Hudson was an injured seaman on the *Doria*. Luckily he woke up just in time and managed to find his way up to the main deck. It took him more than an hour to get up top and he became the very last person to be plucked from danger. Soon afterwards, as many of the horrified survivors looked on, the *Doria* gave a mighty heave and disappeared forever beneath the dark and chilly waters of the North Atlantic.

ANUPAM GAUR
A helicopter in the Himalayas
(India, 2007)

An Italian holds the record for the highest-ever helicopter rescue at 7,800 metres (or nearly five miles above sea level), but one of the most heroic and remarkable feats of mountain flying was carried out in the Himalayan mountains by a colonel in the Indian army.

In 2007 Anupam Gaur was stationed on the Siachen Glacier, which straddles the borders of India, China and Pakistan. The glacier is part of a gigantic ice field covering more than 250 square miles. As a helicopter pilot in the army's Aviation Corps, Anupam's job was to fly supplies into the region as well as looking out for any mountaineers, military or civilian, who were in trouble.

As a young man he had spent a lot of time on the glacier, and had trained there when he first joined the army. The thin mountain air meant it could sometimes be hard to breathe, and temperatures frequently dropped to 50° below freezing. But as a keen pilot Anupam enjoyed the challenges of working in such an extreme environment. He and a group of other pilots ate and slept in a cluster of small fibre-glass huts, but none of them seemed to mind the discomfort.

The thin mountain air meant it could sometimes be hard to breathe

In September a team of experienced, well-equipped mountaineers passed by the huts. Eleven of them were on their way to climb Rimo, one of India's highest peaks at 7,385 metres. One of the pilots advised them to call off the expedition. Rimo was an exceptionally tough climb at any time of the year, even for experts, and all the pilots knew that the weather forecast for the next few weeks was not good.

The mountaineers had been planning their trip for a while so they decided to go on anyway. It was several days before anyone in the huts began to wonder how they had got on. It was worrying that nobody had seen anyone coming back down the mountain, and after ten days there was still no sign of them.

Anupam was sitting in his hut when he received a call on his satellite telephone, a special model designed to work in very remote areas. The caller was one of the mountaineers, who said his group had run into trouble. During the final section of the climb, as they were nearing the peak, a rope had snapped, causing everyone to fall back down a steep slope. Three of them had been injured in the fall and the rest of the group were now in a bad way. They had run out of food and their emergency telephone was almost out of batteries. 'If you don't come soon,' the exhausted mountaineer told Anupam, 'we will all die here.'

It was clear that the mountaineers needed to be evacuated immediately, and as soon as the pilots had permission from their senior officers they loaded supplies of food and water into their helicopters. Several of them took off, but the weather was already turning bad. Visibility was poor due to the snow, and the sheer size of the mountain made things even worse. Rimo has six separate peaks, and even though the pilots knew the area well it took more than an hour to spot the mountaineers huddled together at nearly 5,800 metres.

The deep snow at this height meant it was impossible to land so the pilots decided to drop parcels of food as close as possible to the stranded climbers. Unfortunately, most of the packets sank into the snow and were lost.

After seeing the mountaineers, Anupam and his colleagues realised how serious their injuries were. The men would still be in trouble even if they were able to eat something and get their strength back. One of them had a broken shoulder and two more were so badly frostbitten that they couldn't walk, let alone climb down a mountain.

Because the helicopters couldn't find anywhere safe to land the pilots

had to fly back to their base, which meant the mountaineers would have to spend another day and night in the freezing conditions. Anupam hoped that it would be possible for him to try another rescue the following morning.

Unfortunately the next day the weather was even worse. More snow had fallen overnight and the helicopters' rotor blades kicked this up in clouds, making it even harder for any of the pilots to see what they were doing. However, Anupam knew they had no choice but to try again. Time was running out for the mountaineers and without the army's help they would almost certainly perish.

He decided to fly back up the mountain, but this time with much less fuel. This would limit the amount of time he could stay airborne, but by reducing the weight of the helicopter it might be easier to control it in the thin atmosphere. Anupam's plan was to fly as close as he could to the mountain. If he could hover just a few centimetres above the ground, his co-pilot might be able to pull the injured men into the helicopter. They could then be flown back down to the camp and taken to hospital.

It was a daring plan, and highly dangerous, but it might just work. Flying a helicopter really close to the ground takes enormous skill, even on flat land and in perfect weather. Thousands of metres up a mountain, with snow blowing and high winds, it would be a demanding challenge even for a pilot as skilled and experienced as Anupam Gaur.

It was a daring plan, and highly dangerous but it might just work

Carrying just enough fuel for the journey up to the injured men and back again, Anupam took off. When he spotted the climbers he carefully manoeuvred his helicopter so that it was almost touching the ground.

Hovering is much harder than it looks, but he managed to do it so precisely that one of the helicopter's skis actually rested on top of the snow. The other ski had to be kept airborne in order to prevent the heavy machine sinking into the snow.

Anupam managed to hold this position for long enough for the first of the mountaineers to scramble aboard – his plan was working. The others followed, but it took time because the more seriously injured ones needed a lot of help from the co-pilot. Anupam meanwhile had to struggle with his controls. It was important to keep the helicopter steady as its weight increased from each new passenger coming on board. He also had to make sure he didn't use up all the fuel.

It was important to keep the helicopter steady as its weight increased from each new passenger coming on board

Eventually all eleven mountaineers were taken off the mountain. With the fuel close to running out, Anupam was able to bring the whole group down safely. Several of them needed time in hospital, and a few fingers were lost to frostbite, but Anupam Gaur had managed to rescue the injured climbers and all of their colleagues.

'BUSTER' CAIN
Teenage hero of the Blitz
(England, 1940)

During the Second World War cities across Europe were bombed repeatedly from the air. London was one of the worst affected. Two million homes were damaged or destroyed, along with hundreds of thousands of offices, shops, warehouses and factories. Approximately 32,000 people were killed by enemy action and many more injured in raids which saw hundreds of tonnes of bombs rain down from the skies. These attacks happened every single night, often for weeks on end.

In what became known as the Blitz, loud sirens were used to warn people when the bombers were approaching so that everyone could find somewhere to take cover. Often there were two or three hundred aircraft at a time and many families slept in special air-raid shelters in their gardens or in Underground stations. These were thought to be safer than staying in a house, although the shelters could be cold, damp, cramped and uncomfortable.

Loud sirens were used to warn people when the bombers were approaching

A lot of people were killed immediately in fires and explosions, but others died after becoming trapped in bombed-out buildings. When a building caught fire or was so badly damaged that it collapsed, it was often too dangerous for the police, firemen or specially trained air-raid wardens to go into the ruins looking for survivors.

John Cain lived in east London, which was one of the worst-affected areas. (Many of London's huge docks were situated here, which made it an important target for the bombers.) He was only fifteen years old, but in the 1940s most children left school at fourteen, and John worked on his father's market stall selling fruit and vegetables. John always wore a hat called a trilby when he was working, and he liked to juggle with cabbages. He was quite a cheeky boy, but he was popular with the other stallholders and his father's customers. Everyone called him Buster.

One night in November 1940 an old paint factory close to the market was hit by at least one massive German bomb. The chemicals used in oil paints make them highly flammable, and the building was already burning fiercely by the time Buster rushed over to see what was going on. Four policemen arrived on the scene at about the same time and Buster told them he thought there were people trapped inside.

The people had probably taken shelter in the basement, and it was obvious to everyone that this was a potentially deadly situation. With so many other burning buildings in the area, there was a real risk that the fire brigade might not arrive in time to save any of them.

The only light inside came from burning paint, which was streaming across the floor

The policemen knew this and they decided to enter the building themselves and start a search for survivors. Buster Cain followed them in. The policemen split up into two groups, but finding anyone inside the wrecked building must have seemed like an impossible task. The only light inside came from burning paint, which was streaming across the floor. There were also live wires running from the machines in the factory, and falling bricks and broken glass from the blast. Several times the police and Buster were driven back by the heat and smoke, but they refused to give up.

Eventually, they managed to reach the basement of the burning building where they found the people Buster had told them about. The police knew they had to get them out as quickly as possible. The building looked like it was going to collapse, and having breathed the thick smoke and poisonous paint fumes, several of the victims needed urgent medical treatment. By now more paint was dripping from the floors above and soaking into Buster's clothes and the policemen's uniforms. This was uncomfortable, but it also meant that they were at even greater risk of catching alight.

Desperate to get everyone out as quickly as they could, one of the group suggested using a door and some long planks of wood as stretchers. In this way Buster was able to help the policemen carry the injured out into the street.

Getting everybody clear of the building took a while, but eventually seven people were brought to safety and taken away in ambulances. Shortly afterwards, as the police and Buster gazed up at the burning factory, there was a mighty crash. Moments later almost the entire building collapsed into the basement where they had all been standing just minutes earlier.

Moments later almost the entire building collapsed

Buster seemed very calm about it all. This was probably because, unbelievably, it wasn't the first time he had acted in such a selfless and courageous way. The night before, the boy had been involved in another rescue after several customers became trapped in a burning pub in a nearby street. In fact, Buster is thought to have rescued more than thirty people in all from various bombed-out buildings during the Blitz, although the paint factory was by far the most dangerous. The policeman knew the pub and was very impressed by Buster's coolness and determination. He made a note of Buster's name as the fifteen-year-old wandered off into the night.

By the following morning Buster was back at work with his father selling fruit and juggling vegetables. A few months later he heard that news of his actions that night had reached Buckingham Palace. As a result, he was going to be awarded the George Medal for his bravery.

The medal was named after the king, George VI, and at the time Buster was the youngest person to have one. When he went to the palace to collect it he was still wearing his trilby hat, but he now also had a smart new suit which had been made especially for him by His Majesty's own tailor.

Brian Keaulana and Earl Bungo
A jet-ski to the rescue (Hawaii, 1993)

The American islands of Hawaii are located about 2,000 miles from the USA mainland in the middle of the Pacific Ocean. This part of the world's largest ocean is known for its huge and powerful waves, which make Hawaii a popular destination for surfers. The islanders were riding on simple wooden boards more than 300 years ago, but with 'breakers' reaching more than fifteen metres high it can be incredibly dangerous, even for expert surfers.

In 1993 a twenty-six-year-old tourist called Hugh Alexander was knocked off a high rock by one of these giant waves. He and a friend fell more than six metres into the water. The friend, Katja Teip, was quickly pulled out by a nearby group of soldiers, but Hugh was washed away. He became trapped in a famous sea cave called the Moi Hole, where the soldiers couldn't see him.

With gigantic waves pounding at the entrance to the cave it wasn't a safe place to be. Parts of the cave were dry, but it was filling up with water and there was nothing Hugh could do to get out. He managed to find a tiny crevice in the wall of the cave and crawled into it. In this way he was able to avoid being battered by the waves, but he was still stuck there more than an hour later when Brian Keaulana and Craig Davidson roared up outside on a jet-ski.

It was filling up with water and there was nothing Hugh could do to get out

The jet-ski is a sort of cross between a speedboat and a motorbike. This one belonged to the Hawaii Department of Parks and Recreation, and the two men were employed as water safety officers or lifeguards. Neither of them could see anyone in the rough water, but when they switched off the engine they thought they could hear Hugh's voice from inside the cave. He was calling for help, but they could hardly hear him above the deafening sound of the waves crashing on to the rocks and the noise of a helicopter circling overhead.

Brian and Craig were worried that the power of the waves meant it would be hard, maybe impossible, for even a strong swimmer to get out of the cave on his own. They also knew that Hugh might be injured and that if he wasn't brought out soon he would eventually die of hypothermia. This is a medical condition which occurs when a person gets too cold to move around properly.

While they wondered what to do next, the two officers were themselves hit by another massive wave. This swamped the jet-ski with seawater and Brian was unable to restart the engine. Without any power the men were in danger of being smashed on to the rocks. To avoid this a rope was attached to the jet-ski so it could be towed to safety by the helicopter.

Without any power the men were in danger of being smashed on to the rocks

Craig stayed on board to steer the jet-ski and Brian remained behind to see if there was anything he could do at the cave. His only thought was to put on a pair of fins or flippers. These might be enough to help him swim into the cave and then out again with Hugh. It was a difficult and dangerous plan, but the first part worked well enough. Unfortunately, when Brian got into the cave, he couldn't see the crevice where Hugh was hiding.

Brian was naturally worried about getting trapped in there himself. Three- and four-metre waves were still pounding against the cave walls, and at one point he had to take a deep breath and dive down as deep as he could to avoid being battered by them. He held on to a rock at the bottom of the cave, but eventually had to come back to the surface to take another breath. Finally the danger became too great and, reluctantly, he decided to try and swim back out of the cave while he still had the strength to beat the waves.

Brian's flippers helped him a lot and he soon found himself out of the cave and back in daylight. By now another of his colleagues, a man called Earl Bungo, had turned up on a second jet-ski. The two of them manoeuvred it as close as they could to the rocky entrance and called out to Hugh. However hard it was for Hugh to swim out of the cave, it might be his only chance.

The pair realised that Hugh would be have to be amazingly lucky to pull this off. It was vital that he got his timing right. He needed to make the attempt during a lull between two waves. Brian and Earl, meanwhile, had to get close enough to the entrance to snatch him from the water, but not so close that they and the second jet-ski would be driven on to the rocks.

Hugh's first attempt almost succeeded. For a moment he appeared at the cave entrance, but seconds later he disappeared again as he was knocked backwards by a particularly powerful wave. Brian shouted at him to have another go. Hugh kept trying, but the more tired he got the more unlikely it was that he would have the strength needed to fight his way out of the cave.

After a brief rest Hugh gave it a final go. Once again, during a brief gap between two monster waves, he appeared outside the cave. As Brian accelerated to get the jet-ski as close to him as possible, Earl reached down, grabbed Hugh's arm and hauled him out of the swirling, crashing water.

For a moment it looked like Hugh was safe, but then another wave knocked him off the jet-ski and Earl fell in after him. Now both men were in danger of being washed back into the cave. Choosing his moment carefully, Brian swung the jet-ski around again and powered it back through the waves towards them. He too was becoming exhausted now, but somehow he found the strength to pull both Earl and Hugh back on to the jet-ski. Before the next wave hit them, he gunned the engine again and raced as fast as he could away from the rocks and into the relative safety of the deeper water.

Now both men were in danger of being washed back into the cave

Hugh was shaken, but luckily his injuries weren't serious and he made a full recovery. As the story of his rescue spread, all three lifeguards were treated as heroes in Hawaii. Brian eventually quit his job though, and went on to work as a stuntman on several Hollywood hits including *Jurassic World* and *Dawn of the Planet of the Apes*.

WAYNE SHORTHOUSE
When a daring stunt goes wrong
(England, 2015)

Mike French was a corporal in the Red Devils when his parachute got tangled up in the legs of a fellow soldier.

The men and women of the Parachute Regiment's elite skydiver display team are all serving soldiers in the British army and have seen action in wars around the globe. They have also done thousands of parachute jumps since the team was formed more than fifty years ago. Fortunately, in that time accidents have been very rare, although one of the team broke a leg after landing badly at Wembley Stadium when Manchester United played Everton in the 1985 FA Cup Final.

At the start of a display, the Red Devils usually jump from around 4,000 metres and freefall at a speed of up to 120 miles an hour

At the start of a display, the Red Devils usually jump from around 4,000 metres and freefall at a speed of up to 120 miles an hour. After about forty-five seconds they open their parachutes to slow their descent. As with any parachute jump it can be very dangerous, so like most professionals each member wears a spare or reserve parachute in case the first one doesn't work.

When he got into trouble Mike and his colleagues were taking part in a display at the Whitehaven Air Show in Cumbria. After leaping out of their aeroplane high above the display area the twelve-strong team was planning to perform a stunt called a 'stack'. To prepare for this the skydivers need to fly even closer to each other than they normally do. Then, in order to make the stack, they have to position themselves in very close formation, so close that each team member can place his feet on the parachute canopy of the person below.

Accompanied by spirals and swirls of coloured smoke from special canisters attached to the parachutists' legs, the whole thing looks spectacular from the ground, but it makes the jump even more hazardous than usual. Coming down in such close formation, it takes great skill to avoid endangering another member of the team or becoming tangled up in the lines of someone else's parachute.

This time something went badly wrong. As he drifted down towards the large crowd of excited spectators, Mike's parachute looked like it hadn't opened properly. Moments later he collided with his fellow corporal, Wayne Shorthouse, the Red Devils' display coordinator. Luckily neither of them was injured as they made contact, but there was a very real chance now that one or both of them could plummet hundreds of metres towards the ground.

Falling a lot faster than expected, Mike looked up and could see that part of his parachute had become wrapped around Wayne's legs. It was possible he didn't have enough height left to free himself from the parachute and open the reserve before he hit the ground. Wayne also realised immediately what had happened, and quickly took action. Coming in even closer to his stricken teammate, he struggled to hook one leg

Mike looked up and could see that part of his parachute had become wrapped around Wayne's legs

and then another around the lines of Mike's collapsing parachute.

This was an extremely difficult manoeuvre to pull off, and it was vital he got it right. If he didn't there would be a horrible accident. Both men knew that this close to the ground Mike had no other options – and that time was running out fast.

Thankfully Wayne managed to get both of his legs into Mike's lines pretty quickly, and he now held on as tightly as he could. With only one working parachute between them the combined weight of the two men meant they were still coming down a lot faster than in a conventional jump. Even so, it was possible for them to land safely, and Wayne was confident that, as long as he could maintain his grip on Mike's lines with his legs, he could keep them both out of trouble.

With Mike shouting instructions from below, the whole drama had taken just a few moments to unfold, but to the spectators on the ground it looked horrifying. For several seconds no one could really tell what was going on up there. First one man and then two appeared to be in trouble, and it must have been obvious to anyone watching that they were falling much faster than usual.

> The whole drama had taken just a few moments to unfold, but to the spectators on the ground it looked horrifying

Fortunately, while panic spread quickly through the crowd of spectators, Wayne managed to keep calm. Holding on to Mike's parachute, he used his own canopy to steer away from the public below. A few moments later the two men splashed down safely in the chilly water of a nearby yacht marina.

As soon as everyone realised the pair were unharmed a huge cheer went up from the crowd. In a matter of seconds, the mood of excitement and anticipation had turned to horror and then genuine relief as a potential tragedy had been averted.

Talking afterwards about what had happened, the two Red Devils seemed strangely relaxed, perhaps because they knew how rare this sort of incident is. As soon as he had climbed out of the water and dried off, Wayne Shorthouse was insisting that he wasn't a hero. According to him, he was only doing his job when his cool head, strong legs and quick thinking had saved Mike's life.

There also wasn't much talk of danger, from either Wayne or Mike. It is possible that the whole thing happened so quickly that neither of them had had time to think about how bad it might have been. According to Wayne the success of the rescue was all down to their experience and their military

training. Between them the pair have made more than 6,000 jumps and have worked together for years. On the rare occasions when something goes wrong professional soldiers are trained to focus on the job in hand, to remember what they've been taught and to react quickly.

RESHMA BEGUM
Two weeks trapped under rubble (Bangladesh, 2013)

More than a thousand people died when a gigantic factory collapsed in one of the world's worst ever industrial disasters. The Rana Plaza factory was situated on the outskirts of Dhaka, the capital of Bangladesh. The workers employed in the factory made clothes for companies in Europe and America.

Around two thousand of them managed to escape from the building, but 1,134 lives were lost. The victims were killed by falling rubble or died after becoming trapped beneath hundreds of tonnes of metal, glass and concrete. Tragically, the dead included many small children who had been playing in the building while their mothers worked upstairs as seamstresses sewing clothes.

Witnesses said it took less than ninety seconds for the eight-storey building to crash to the ground. The noise of the collapse was incredible and echoed around the city. Within minutes of the disaster, soldiers, police and firemen were racing to the scene together with many ordinary Bangladeshis.

It took less than ninety seconds for the eight-storey building to crash to the ground

There wasn't much to see through the clouds of choking dust and smoke, but they could hear the terrified voices of people buried under the rubble. Some of the victims were crying out for someone to come and help them. Others were using their mobile phones, making desperate calls to family members and loved ones. Many were horribly injured and later died.

Teams of volunteers immediately began searching through the rubble, removing lumps of masonry piece by piece. It was hard work and it had to be done by hand because the rescuers didn't have any machinery to help them. Doing it this way was also slow, but it was probably safer than using heavy equipment. Diggers and bulldozers can move more rubble more quickly, but they can cause additional injuries by accidentally dislodging unstable sections of wall or ceiling. This sort of machine is also very noisy, which makes it hard for searchers to hear any cries for help, or the sound of people tapping on walls or pipes to draw attention to their location.

The rescue teams found mostly dead bodies, hundreds of them, while they searched through the remains of the factory, but sometimes they got lucky. For example, after two full days of searching, twenty-four people were brought out safely. A fireman had heard the sound of someone hitting a metal pipe with a brick repeatedly. By following the sound he made his way towards a group of survivors who were trapped in a sort of cavern or air pocket on what had been the third floor.

Several of the group were quite badly injured, but they were all alive. Unfortunately most of the other discoveries were grim. Soon the bodies of the dead began to decompose in the heat of Bangladesh's tropical climate. As the days passed, fewer and fewer people were pulled alive from the ruins. Slowly those family members who had come to help began to realise that any of their relatives still buried under the building were probably now dead.

Some of those in charge of the rescue thought it was time to stop looking for survivors. They wanted bulldozers to be brought in to clear the site so that the factory could be rebuilt. But others argued against this and demanded that the rescue operation carry on. Relatives of the missing workers were desperate for the volunteers to keep searching.

Relatives of the missing workers were desperate for the volunteers to keep searching

Abdur Razzaq was one of those who kept on looking, and he was still at it more than two weeks after the building had collapsed. He was a sergeant in the Bangladeshi army and spent each day and much of the night shifting rubble and searching for survivors. By the seventeenth day no one was hearing voices any more, but that afternoon Abdur thought he could hear something from deep inside the giant pile.

It sounded a bit like ticking, a metallic tapping that was so quiet he thought he might be imagining it. Just in case it was real, Abdur got down

on his hands and knees and listened intently. Now he could definitely hear something. It was faint but it was there again. Tap, tap. Tap, tap.

Excitedly Abdur kept his ear close to the ground, listening out for something more. Suddenly he heard a voice. It was very quiet, like the tapping had been, but he was sure he could hear something, a whisper. Soon he had no doubt: it was the voice of a woman asking him for help.

Soon he had no doubt: it was the voice of a woman asking him for help

Carefully, but as fast as he dared, Abdur began pulling away at jagged pieces of the wreckage. Colleagues joined him and soon, to their surprise and delight, they found a nineteen-year-old called Reshma Begum. No one had been found alive for several days, but this showed that Abdur had been right to keep on searching through the ruins.

Reshma had been working on the second floor of the factory when disaster struck. She was buried under a huge pile of clothes when the floor beneath her collapsed. The soft material might have saved her life because in those first few seconds several friends working nearby had been killed. Reshma was unharmed, but she had become trapped between the one of the building's beams and a column that was meant to support the ceiling.

She found she had a tiny space to move around in, but there was no light to see anything and she couldn't find a way out. Feeling her way around in the darkness, she had been able to scavenge some food. Mostly this came from bags that had belonged to her dead friends. She'd also found some small plastic bottles full of water. Although she was very thirsty she drank only a tiny amount each day. It was just enough for her to avoid becoming dehydrated, but the last bottle had run out by the fourteenth day.

During that time, as more and more of the rubble was lifted away, Reshma had begun to hear the sound of people moving around above her. She soon realised, however, that none of them could hear her, not even when she started banging on a block of concrete with a piece of metal pipe. The pipe was something else she had found lying in the darkness. When she wasn't hitting the concrete with it she used it to breathe through, poking it through a gap in the rubble when her air began to run out.

She started banging on a block of concrete with a piece of metal pipe

Reshma didn't think she had any serious injuries but, after so long trapped and alone in the dark, she had begun to panic. By the sixteenth day she thought she would never be rescued and would die like so many others. Thankfully, the following day, Abdur had a heard the sound of her banging. Finally she was able to hear the sound of a handsaw, and then welding and drilling equipment as rescuers cut through the steel and concrete that was holding her prisoner.

Eventually the rescuers reached her and Reshma Begum was brought out on a stretcher and taken off to hospital. The teenager was lucky enough to make a full recovery, but sadly she was the very last person to be found alive in the building.

CHESLEY SULLENBERGER
An emergency landing on water (USA, 2009)

Because so many of us jet off on holiday it's easy to forget how dangerous flying can be. Something as small as a bird can cause even a large, modern aeroplane to crash if it gets sucked into one of the engines.

This is what happened in January 2009 to US Airways Flight 1549, an Airbus A320 carrying 150 passengers and five crew. The incident happened on the way from New York to Charlotte Douglas International Airport in the state of North Carolina.

The journey down to North Carolina should have taken around two hours, but disaster struck in the first few minutes. Shortly after taking off, the aircraft was already flying at 230 miles an hour about a thousand metres above New York. Suddenly, it was hit by a flock of Canada geese. A couple of the birds got caught in its two engines and were killed immediately. A goose weighs only five or six kilograms, but this is more than enough to wreck the engines of a seventy-tonne aircraft. Within seconds of this happening, Flight 1549's pilot, Chesley 'Sully' Sullenberger, realised that both of his engines had stopped working.

A goose weighs only five or six kilograms, but this is more than enough to wreck the engines of a seventy-tonne aircraft

Most aircraft will glide for a short while without any power, even a big, heavy one like the A320. Sully and his co-pilot Jeff Skiles struggled to restart one or other of the engines, but they were too badly damaged for this. Both had shut down, so the pilot sent a radio message to the air traffic control tower at New York's LaGuardia Airport. The message said they were turning back immediately and needed to make an emergency landing.

The two runways at the airport were quickly cleared of other aircraft, and several fire trucks moved into position in case the A320 caught fire as it landed. Sully was one of the airline's most experienced pilots, but in more than forty years of flying this had never happened to him before. The former fighter pilot knew he had to think and act fast. Every second counted.

Sully soon realised that he wouldn't be able to turn and glide all the way back to LaGuardia without any power from the engines. He briefly considered trying to reach a smaller airport that was closer, but then radioed again to say he didn't think the aircraft could make it to this one either.

With the A320 now losing height, there was no time to come up with another plan. Sully radioed the tower a third time to say that his aircraft was going to come down in the Hudson River. Pilots call it a 'deadstick landing' when they have to land without engine power. It is extremely difficult to do safely and landing in water makes it much harder, and even more dangerous. Sully told his passengers to get ready for the impact, and prepared to ditch the plane in the wide Hudson River.

He knew he couldn't just splash down as fast as possible. If he did, the heavy plane would sink before any of the passengers had time to get out. Also, the massive George Washington Bridge was blocking his path. More than 180 metres tall and 1,450 metres long, this is the busiest road bridge in the world. It carries fourteen lanes of traffic over the river and is used by more than a hundred million vehicles a year. If Sully hit the bridge it would almost certainly kill everyone on the plane along with countless others driving their cars, buses and trucks.

Controlling such a large aeroplane without the engines is possible, but it takes great skill. Sully needed all his expertise to avoid smashing into the bridge's towering steel structure. He also needed a lot of luck. Even if he managed to miss the bridge, it was important to land the plane on the water as flat as possible. If the huge A320 came down at too much of an angle, it could break up on impact or sink really quickly.

Sully needed all his expertise to avoid smashing into the bridge's towering steel structure

While Sully wrestled with his controls, LaGuardia's air traffic controllers contacted the US Coast Guard to tell them what was happening. The Coast Guard were ordered to clear as many boats as possible from the river, and to get ready to rescue the 155 people on board the plane.

There was almost no time to do this. Just a minute and a half later, Flight 1549, still travelling at around 140 miles an hour, splashed down into the middle of the Hudson. One engine was ripped off instantly as the jet hit the water, but thanks to Sully's brilliant flying the body and wings remained largely intact. Opening his cockpit door into the cabin, Sully ordered an immediate evacuation. The seventy-tonne aircraft was bound to sink – it was just a matter of when it did and how quickly it would go down.

One engine was ripped off instantly as the jet hit the water

As water rushed in through a hole in the fuselage, terrified passengers began clambering out through the four emergency exits as quickly as they could. Once outside, many of them crowded on to the wings and waited to be picked up by rescue boats. Others jumped into the freezing winter water, or used the plane's inflatable emergency slides as makeshift life rafts. A few more tried to swim away, scared that the damaged plane might be about to explode.

The interior of the cabin was now filling up with water very quickly indeed. Scully and his crew instructed those passengers who were still inside to climb over the seats towards the exits, and to do this as fast as they could. Very soon, with help from the flight attendants, everyone was brought out safely, including one passenger with a wheelchair. By now the plane was sitting dangerously low in the water, but Sully refused to leave before he had waded the length of the cabin twice. As captain, he was determined

to make absolutely sure that all his passengers and crew were out before saving himself.

By the time Sully appeared outside the plane, most of the passengers were already on board the many large and small boats which had rushed to the scene to help. By the following morning New Yorkers were describing what had happened as the 'Miracle on the Hudson'. Two passengers had spent a night in hospital, and one of the flight attendants had hurt her leg. But despite the enormity of what had happened, all the other injuries were minor and no one had died.

OPERATION JERICHO
A daring rescue from an enemy jail (France, 1944)

In 1940, during the early part of the Second World War, France was occupied by the German army. After an invasion which took only six weeks to complete, several thousand courageous French men and women became agents of the Resistance movement and went into hiding.

Determined to free their country from German control, the agents' work was secretive and incredibly dangerous. Many members of the Resistance were killed fighting the enemy. Others died while sabotaging military bases or blowing up strategically important railway lines. Large numbers of them were captured and tortured to reveal details of their missions, and sometimes they were even executed by firing squads. By 1943 hundreds had been imprisoned in France and Germany, including dozens who were held captive in the large prison at Amiens, about seventy-five miles north of Paris.

Many members of the Resistance were killed fighting the enemy

In December of that year, twelve of the prisoners at Amiens were executed. There were fears that another hundred or more would be murdered if they refused to reveal the names and hiding places of spies and other people working to free France. In an attempt to prevent this happening, an audacious rescue plan was hatched in Britain. It was to be carried out by pilots and aircraft based at RAF Hunsdon, a small airfield on the border of Essex and Hertfordshire.

Many of the prison inmates were important members of the Resistance so the place was strong and very well guarded. A conventional escape looked unlikely to succeed, and there was no question of sending British troops so far behind enemy lines. Instead a surprise attack from the air was thought to be the best way to attempt a rescue. By the start of the New Year, top-secret plans had been drawn up for an airborne assault on Amiens. The authorities agreed to launch this as soon as possible, before another mass execution took place.

Most of the aircraft based at RAF Hunsdon were of a type called the De Havilland Mosquito. The Mosquito was mostly made of wood rather than metal, but it was a highly effective fighter-bomber. It was fast, sleek and exceptionally manoeuvrable, and the pilots called it the 'Wooden Wonder'. This made it perfect for the sort of low-level flying and accurate, precision bombing that would be needed for a successful assault on the main gates of the prison.

The rescue plan was codenamed 'Operation Jericho' and it involved nearly twenty Mosquito aircraft. Each of them carried two people: a pilot and a navigator. Most of those chosen for the dangerous mission were British, but the raid also included crews from Australia and New Zealand. To begin with, no one at Hunsdon knew the purpose of the mission, not even the pilots. Because of the need for secrecy they were only told the name of the target at eight o'clock on the morning of the raid.

> **The rescue plan was codenamed 'Operation Jericho'**

At the last possible moment the pilots were told that they would have to cross the English Channel and then fly as low as possible over the fields of northern France. Flying just ten metres above the ground (and at 350 miles an hour) would be difficult and dangerous, but it would reduce the chance of the aircraft being spotted on German radar screens. Doing it this way required immense skill and bravery from the pilots, but everything possible had to be done to ensure that the attack came as a surprise.

Unexpectedly awful weather delayed the take-off that morning, and several of the aircraft had to turn back over the Channel. Heavy snow over France made visibility very poor, but the first five crews swooped down on Amiens more or less on schedule at one minute past midday. Two of the Mosquitos attacked a nearby railway station (as a cover for their real mission

and to cause confusion among the Germans). While they did this the other three dropped their powerful high-explosive bombs on to the prison walls.

More Mosquitos soon appeared over the jail, and the ferocious attack continued for several minutes. Each bomb weighed 230 kilograms and between them the Mosquito crews managed to blow a huge hole in the high, snow-covered walls. Another bomb caused a massive fire in the main guardhouse. This was intended to stop the Germans inside from shooting at the 200 or more prisoners who were now trying to make their escape.

From the air it looked like the rescue plan was going well, although the mission didn't involve any of the Mosquitos landing to collect the escaped prisoners. Anyone who got out of the prison just had to run for it. Having dropped their bombs, the pilots had orders to fly home as quickly as possible.

Anyone who got out of the prison just had to run for it

They were not out of danger yet, however. The Germans had ordered their own fighters into the air as soon as they had realised the prison was under attack. One of these, a Focke Wulf 190, managed to shoot down a Mosquito almost immediately. The mission commander, Group Captain Pickard, was killed instantly along with Bill Broadley, his navigator. Two more Mosquitos similarly never made it back to England, and a fourth aircraft was so badly damaged by gunfire that it crashed on the runway while trying to land.

Happily the two New Zealand airmen on board that one were not injured, but three airmen had been killed in the raid and another three were taken prisoner. This was a risky and dangerous mission from the outset, but the deaths were still very shocking to everyone back at Hunsdon. Several of the prisoners died as well, after being shot by the guards or as a result of the exploding bombs. But 258 ran from the prison, including approximately eighty members of the Resistance.

Unfortunately not all of them stayed free for long: some had been injured in the blast and were recaptured before they had got very far. But many were successful and were able to go back into hiding. This meant the Resistance could continue its important work, attacking the enemy and paving the way for the D-Day landings and the eventual liberation of France later on that year.

MOHAMMED OMAR AL SHAMMA AND MUSTAFA AHMED MOHAMMED

Trapped in a burning building (Saudi Arabia, 2012)

When an apartment block in the Red Sea port of Jeddah caught fire, two firefighters were beaten back by the flames and seriously injured. In a big city with a population of more than four million, fires like this happen all the time, but this one was particularly serious. The blaze had been caused by a gas explosion, and an eleven-year-old boy was trapped in a room on one of the upper floors.

Before the firemen had even got there, people watching from across the street noticed how quickly the fire was spreading. Great clouds of pungent black smoke had begun billowing from one side of the building and flames five metres high were leaping from the walls.

We like to think we would help someone in danger, but when something as frightening as this happens most people stand around watching because they don't know what to do. Sometimes rescue attempts are best left to professionals, the people who have been trained to deal with this sort of incident and who know the best way to approach the scene of a disaster.

Unfortunately on that day in Jeddah it wasn't possible to wait for the experts to arrive. The fire was spreading incredibly quickly and it was obvious to many watching that the building wouldn't last long. Clearly the boy needed to be rescued as quickly as possible, but most of the onlookers were too scared even to cross the street.

Most of the onlookers were too scared even to cross the street

Despite the searing heat and the obvious dangers, two brave teenagers decided they would have a go at rescuing him themselves. Mohammed Omar Al Shamma was born in Saudi Arabia, but Mustafa Ahmed Mohammed had moved to Jeddah from Chad in central Africa. Neither of them had any training for this kind of thing. They didn't even have a ladder. They were just two ordinary young men who knew they had to do something, and do it quickly.

Mohammed and Mustafa guessed that by now it wouldn't be possible for them to just run up the stairs. The fire had already been raging for several minutes, but the pair were confident they could reach the boy by climbing up the outside of the sand-coloured apartment building. This wouldn't be easy, but it seemed to be their best option even though they probably hadn't worked out yet how they were going to get the little boy back down to the ground.

Climbing up a vertical wall would be quite dangerous even without the smoke and flames. But they were both young and fit, and it didn't take them long to reach the second floor. Soon they were perched, standing upright, on a narrow brick ledge.

This ran along one side of the house. It was only a few inches wide and they had to grip the rough bricks with their fingertips so they wouldn't fall off. As quickly as they could, the pair edged towards the window where they had seen the boy crying for help. When they peered through the glass they could see he was still there. He wasn't injured, but he was unable to open the window.

They had to grip the rough bricks with their fingertips so they wouldn't fall off

Mohammed and Mustafa couldn't open it either, not from outside. One of them gestured frantically to the boy, shouting at him to move a couple of metres back into the room. They had decided to smash the glass so it was important that the child was not standing anywhere near. There was also a risk that they would accidentally make the fire even worse. Breaking the window would let more air into the building, which would feed the flames.

Modern plate glass is surprisingly strong, and Mohammed and Mustafa didn't have anything with them which they could use to smash it. Also each of them had only one hand free to do this. They needed their other hands to steady themselves on the narrow ledge.

It took a few moments but, after several attempts, the two were able to break the glass. Mohammed and Mustafa carefully lifted the boy over the shattered edges of the window, and pulled him out through the frame. Fortunately, someone down below had managed to find a ladder and moved it into position. As the teenagers brought the boy down the large crowd began to clap and cheer. The building carried on burning, but the child was safe.

Dave Hahn
His helicopter crashes but he carries on (USA, 2002)

Dave Hahn is a professional mountain guide and climber, and one of America's most famous mountaineers. He's climbed to the top of Mount Everest fifteen times and has reached the summit of the highest mountain in Antarctica more than twenty times. In 1999, during yet another trip up Everest, he discovered the body of George Mallory, who had disappeared there three-quarters of a century earlier.

George Mallory was a young Englishman who led the first ever expedition to conquer the world's tallest mountain. Altogether he made four attempts on the summit. Dave found frozen human remains buried in snow near the top, at 8,200 metres. These were identified as George's, but it was impossible to say whether he and his climbing partner Andrew Irvine had died on their way up or on the way down.

It was an amazing, if gruesome, discovery and since making it Dave has gone on to break many important climbing records. He has also won numerous awards, but is probably best known for an audacious rescue which he carried out on an American mountain in 2002 – and for his astonishing escape earlier the same day.

Both incidents happened on Mount Rainier in Washington State, a mountain Dave knows very well because he has climbed it more than 270 times. It's nowhere near as tall as Everest, but it's one of America's highest and most challenging peaks. Even experienced mountaineers admit that it is one of the most dangerous climbs anywhere on that continent.

The weather at any height can be very unpredictable and even in August the temperature at the summit rarely rises above freezing point. There are two volcanic craters near the top of the mountain, and more than thirty-six square miles of its slopes are covered in snow and ice all year round. Much of the ice formed millions of years ago into twenty-six massive glaciers. Some of these are America's largest outside Alaska.

The weather at any height can be very unpredictable

In a typical year at least two climbers are killed in this hazardous environment, and in 1981 a group of eleven perished in a single ice fall. More recently another party of six mountaineers all died attempting to reach its 4,392-metre summit. On that occasion the dead included two experienced, professional guides who had both climbed Mount Rainier many times. Three of the bodies have still not been found.

In 2002 Dave was asked to help with a particularly difficult rescue. A nineteen-year-old called Jesse Whitcomb had been climbing with his father and a friend when he'd sustained a serious head injury. The three had set off for the summit in good weather and they were all expert mountaineers. Their preparations for the climb had been good, and they were well equipped with some of the best gear. Unfortunately a falling boulder had crashed down on to one of them and now they were stuck.

The rock had probably been dislodged by melting snow and ice, and it had hit Jesse with considerable force. As well as smashing his protective helmet, it knocked him out and Jesse tumbled thirty metres down a steep slope.

Unfortunately a falling boulder had crashed down on to one of them and now they were stuck

Although he was quite young Jesse had climbed Rainier once before, but now he was stranded at around 2,865 metres. He had recovered consciousness after about five minutes, but he had a deep cut on his neck, his back hurt and his father realised he needed urgent medical attention. When Dave and a climbing ranger called Chris Olson heard this, they knew it was important to reach him as quickly as possible. Grabbing their own equipment, they jumped into a four-seat rescue helicopter.

Flying at 120 miles an hour, a helicopter like the Bell Jet Ranger can often be the quickest way to reach the top of a mountain. However, flying in the mountains can be just as hazardous as climbing, and sometimes even worse.

Poor visibility can cause huge problems for the pilot, but there are many other difficulties too and at least one trained mountain guide has been killed on Rainier while assisting with just this kind of rescue. Tragically, he died after slipping more than a thousand metres down the mountain while trying to help an injured climber into the helicopter. Because there are so many risks, these expensive machines are used to rescue climbers only in genuine medical emergencies and when every other alternative has been considered and ruled out.

Even with the most experienced pilot things can go very wrong very

There was a loud bang and it suddenly went into a violent spin

quickly. As the helicopter carrying Dave and Chris made its way towards a part of the mountain called Liberty Ridge, there was a loud bang and it suddenly went into a violent spin. While it had been hovering close to the ground, the helicopter's tail rotor had struck the ground in an area known as the Carbon Glacier. The pilot lost control and it was obvious at once that it was going to crash. Within seconds, the Jet Ranger came down hard.

All three men thought they were going to die but, remarkably, after climbing out of the wreckage, neither Dave nor the pilot was even slightly injured. Chris wasn't either and had probably had the luckiest escape. He'd managed to duck just as the Jet Ranger's heavy steel gearbox came crashing through the roof. The men later discovered that theirs was one of three helicopter crashes in the mountains that month.

On this occasion they were lucky enough to walk away, but everyone was badly shaken by the experience. The helicopter had crashed nose-down in the snow. With a broken tail and snapped rotor blades, the mangled wreck was now completely useless.

With a broken tail and snapped rotor blades, the mangled wreck was now completely useless

As there was no question of it taking off again, Dave and Chris waited until another, much larger military helicopter called a Chinook arrived to take the pilot back down the mountain. Under the circumstances no one would have blamed either of them for getting on board and going home themselves. However, Jesse still needed their help. Neither of the men was going to let a small thing like a helicopter crash put them off their original objective.

After pulling their mountaineering gear and emergency medical equipment out of the wreckage, Dave and Chris set off up the glacier to the place where Jesse was stranded. Even on a good day it would have been a gruelling climb. There were numerous ice- and rock-fall hazards along the way, and a deadly crevasse (a crack in the surface of the glacier) which they had to get across safely.

While they continued to climb, the Chinook made its way back up the mountain in another attempt to reach the injured climber. On board were members of a second rescue team who had to be lowered down to Jesse by cable because there was nowhere safe for the helicopter to land. The quickest thing would have been to winch Jesse up to safety using the same cable. Unfortunately he was much too ill for this so instead he was placed on a stretcher while they waited for Dave and Chris to arrive.

With the weather closing in, the journey from the crash site took the pair several hours, but eventually Dave and Chris reached Jesse. With help from the second team they were able, very carefully, to lower him several hundred metres back down the glacier where they found a place the Chinook could land safely. From there it took only a few minutes to get everyone on board and soon Jesse was on his way to an army medical centre.

The rescue had taken more than ten hours, six men, two pilots and a helicopter crash – but the three climbers were safe and Jesse made a full recovery.

Eddie Hall
Just doing his job
(USA, 2013)

Shana Porter was driving to work one morning when her car was involved in a collision with a taxi on a busy interstate highway. After crashing off the road into a concrete barrier and tumbling down an embankment, her Honda Accord hit a tree and then a fence. Moments later it burst into flames. Luckily two women motorists who were passing had seen the accident happen. They pulled over and tried to get Shana out of the car, but they were quickly beaten back by the heat and the ferocity of the fire.

Both women ran back up to the road in the hope that they could get another motorist to stop and help them get Shana out. The first person they saw was Eddie Hall in his white van. Luckily for Shana, Eddie worked as an installer for a local fire safety company. When one of the women asked him if he had a fire extinguisher in the back of his van Eddie told her that he had more than a dozen of them as he was on his way to a job.

In fact, Eddie had already been slowing down as he approached the scene of the accident. He hadn't seen the actual collision, but he could tell that something was wrong and when he switched off his engine he could hear someone screaming. Now, as he got closer to the badly damaged Honda, he could see Shana inside it. She was yelling loudly and had one arm through the open sunroof.

Flames were leaping up from the car's engine

Flames were leaping up from the car's engine and there were clouds of thick grey smoke pouring out of the car. Eddie thought the flames were at least a metre high, making this one of the worst fires he had ever experienced.

It's quite unusual for a modern car to catch fire, but when one does the fuel in its tank means the resulting blaze can get out of control very quickly. Eddie ran back to his van as fast as he could, opened the door at the rear and started pulling out his fire extinguishers.

By now several other motorists had stopped at the scene of the accident and Eddie started yelling at them to grab one of the extinguishers. Several did so and with Eddie shouting instructions they began to direct the jets from the extinguishers on to the burning Honda.

As an expert, Eddie knew that the best way to tackle any fire is to aim the jet at the base of the flames. Unfortunately, standing on the embankment they could only spray down on to the top of the car. Doing it this way was better than doing nothing, but Eddie didn't think it would put out the flames quickly enough to save Shana. He couldn't see a way to get around to the other side of the car either, not without endangering himself or one of the other volunteers.

Eddie was wondering what more he could do when a couple of police cars drove up on a smaller road at the bottom of the embankment. From down there, on the other side of Shana's car, the policemen were in a far better position to fight the fire more effectively.

The officers started spraying at once, but unfortunately police cars in America usually carry only one fire extinguisher each. This meant the police didn't have enough equipment to deal with what was now a raging inferno and they quickly ran dry. When this happened, Shana was still trapped and the Honda was still ablaze.

Shana was still trapped and the Honda was still ablaze

Luckily Eddie had plenty of extinguishers on the ground by his van, and they were mostly large ones. Shouting a warning to the officers, he started hurling the heavy cylinders over the top of the burning car. The police grabbed them and directed them on to the fire. Before long it was brought under control and eventually it was put out. In all, eighteen extinguishers had been needed, and most of them came from Eddie's van.

It still wasn't possible to remove Shana from the car, but now the fire was dealt with she was out of immediate danger. She had to be cut free of the vehicle, and was taken to hospital with burns and a broken leg. Eddie was quite modest about the part he had played in her rescue. He said he was just a fire safety professional doing his job, but the police were in no doubt that his arrival on the scene had made all the difference. A van showing up full of extinguishers was extraordinarily lucky, but it took a hero who knew what to do with them to save Shana's life.

GUSTAVO BADILLO

Lost in a cave and running out of air (Venezuela, 1991)

Cave diving is a popular hobby and can be very exciting, but it is hard to think of a more dangerous way to spend the weekend.

Dry potholing or caving is risky enough. No daylight reaches into the deepest caves, rock falls are common in their narrow passageways, and cavers sometimes need to squeeze through tiny gaps in solid rock. Even the most experienced explorers can become confused or disorientated in large networks of caverns or cave systems, and occasionally someone gets lost and dies down in the dark.

Cave divers face all these risks and more. Wearing bulky breathing equipment makes it harder for them to move around, and it increases the chances of getting trapped underground. Swimming in often freezing cold water is made even more hazardous by strange, unpredictable currents. And there is always the danger that a diver will run out of air before he or she reaches the surface and gets out safely.

There is always the danger that a diver will run out of air before he or she reaches the surface

In 1991 Gustavo Badillo was exploring a famous cave in a South American jungle with his diving partner, Eduardo Wallis. The cave was called the Riito de Acarite. They had heard of it from an account by an English diver who said he had followed a stream running through it to a large subterranean lake. The two friends wanted to find the lake and so they set off to look for it one Saturday evening, wearing wetsuits, rubber fins and scuba gear.

Gustavo was a fully trained diving instructor, but most of his experience involved swimming in the open ocean rather than deep underground. He had a waterproof map to guide them through the cave, and fifty metres of rope, which he tied up at the entrance to the cave. The rope was there to help the two men find their way back to their friends who were waiting for them outside the cave.

The pair swam along for a while until the stream disappeared beneath a ledge of solid rock. Then they had to swim under the water, using their scuba gear to breathe. After a short while they came up into a pocket of air in a small, dark cavern. Here they could breathe naturally, but it was worrying because the little cavern wasn't shown anywhere on their map. This meant the map was wrong (or at least unreliable), so they decided to return to the cave entrance as quickly as possible.

Although both men were wearing lights to illuminate their route they now found they couldn't see anything when they put their heads underwater. Their fins had kicked up a lot of mud as they swam into the cave and this had turned the water a thick, cloudy brown. Also, when Gustavo pulled on the rope which was meant to guide them back, it was loose in his hands. It looked like it hadn't been tied securely enough at the entrance to the cave, which meant it was useless.

Keen to get out, Eduardo felt his way along in the dark and was lucky enough to find a rock passage up to the surface. He was soon safe, but after several minutes there was no sign of Gustavo. Eduardo dived back into the stream to look for him, but he still couldn't see anything through the cloudy water. He couldn't find the passage he had used to escape either, so he came back out of the cave alone.

He was soon safe, but after several minutes there was no sign of Gustavo

Down below, in the dark, Gustavo had also tried to feel his way out, but he'd quickly got lost. Briefly he had become tangled up in the rope although he managed to free himself after a few tense moments. From his dive training he knew it was important not to panic. After resting for a few minutes in another air pocket, Gustavo set out to explore the cave as methodically as possible in the hope that he would find a way out.

However, each time Gustavo dived back into the water and swam along one of the passages he found it was a dead end, or blocked by fallen rocks.

He marked the passage with a cross each time this happened. That way he could make sure he didn't waste time, or the dwindling supply of air in his tank, by going down the same passage twice. He dived again and again but he still couldn't find a way out.

After several hours Gustavo was exhausted. His air supply was running low and he knew the batteries in his lights wouldn't last forever either. Soon only one light was working, so he switched it off to save power and sat shivering on a muddy, slime-covered rock, wondering what to do next. In despair he shouted out to his friends up on the surface, but no one could hear him. For the first time Gustavo began to think he might die down here, in the cold and the dark and all alone.

In despair he shouted out to his friends up on the surface, but no one could hear him

Gustavo didn't know that Eduardo and his other friends were desperately trying to get help. They had contacted two expert cave divers, Americans Steve Gerrard and John Orlowski, who were more than 1,500 miles away. Gustavo had already been missing for thirteen hours by the time they got the call, so it was entirely possible that he might be dead by the time they arrived. Even so, both men were prepared to risk their own lives to recover his body.

It took several hours for their plane to fly down to Venezuela, and after landing the two men were planning to use a helicopter to reach Riito de Acarite as quickly as possible. Unfortunately bad weather meant the helicopter couldn't take off. Steve and John had to travel through the jungle in a Jeep instead, which took even longer than their flight from Florida. By the time the pair made it through with their heavy diving equipment,

Gustavo had spent two nights underground.

The divers had resigned themselves to the fact that they were unlikely to find Gustavo alive and Steve was beginning to worry about how they would get his body out. Depending on time of death, Gustavo's body would have stiffened up, making it much harder to move. It could even have swollen up with gas as part of the normal process of decomposition. Privately Steve wasn't even sure he and John would be able to find the body, but he didn't say anything to Eduardo and the friends who were still waiting nervously at the entrance to the cave.

Steve and John put on their protective wetsuits, and two metal air tanks each. In cave diving it's always important to be prepared for the worst, and neither of them knew how long this would take. Both men entered the cave and, hoping for the best, made their way slowly along the stream.

Once again the visibility was so poor in the muddy water that Steve could barely see John's fins as he followed just a metre behind. Their powerful lights were almost useless so the two men felt their way along the slime-covered walls. Eventually they came to an air pocket, but there was no sign of Gustavo anywhere. They kept going, deeper and deeper into the cave.

The two men felt their way along the slime-covered walls

The further they went in the more the passageway narrowed until it was so tight that John could feel his air tanks scraping along the rocks above his head. After a while he was feeling slightly disorientated too. As he began to surface in another small air pocket he thought he saw a flickering light up ahead. He guessed that he must have somehow turned around and begun swimming back towards Steve.

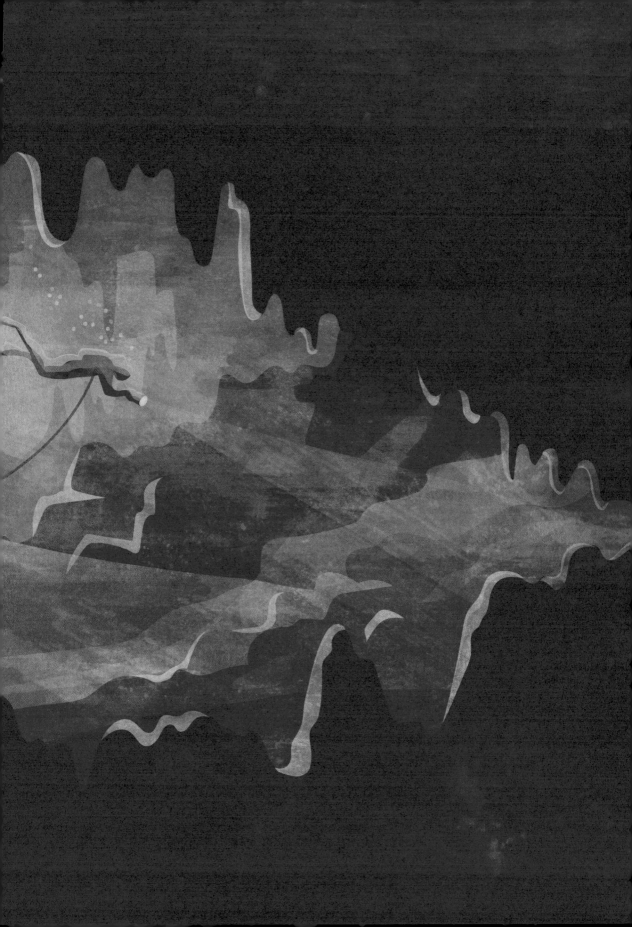

The light was very dim though, and this puzzled him. John and Steve had checked all their equipment several times, and had plenty of batteries. John was confused and put his head above the surface of the water to have a better look. To his astonishment he came face to face with an exhausted Gustavo who was squatting on the slippery rock. When Steve arrived moments later he couldn't believe what he was seeing.

He assumed he had died and that they were angels

Neither could Gustavo, who later admitted that when he first saw the Americans' lights under the water he assumed he had died and that they were angels.

After so long underground Gustavo was dangerously dehydrated. He was also too weak to move, so Steve swam as fast as he could back out of the cave to get some emergency rations while John stayed behind to take care of Gustavo. When Steve returned he had an energy drink and an idea about how to get Gustavo out. While Gustavo recovered some of his strength, Steve showed him how to breathe using air supplied through a long hose attached to one of John's tanks. The three men would then make their way up to the surface, with John leading and Steve bringing up the rear.

After all the waiting it didn't take that long to get the exhausted diver to safety and he was soon back with Eduardo and their friends. It turned out that, sitting on his own in the dark, Gustavo had lost all track of time. He was astonished to discover that it was Monday, the day after *the day after* he and his friend had first dived into the cave.

FLIGHT 251

A crash in the desert
(Mauritania, 1952)

In the 1950s the Handley Page Hermes was one of the world's most advanced airliners. It was based on a wartime bomber called the Halifax, but could fly higher and travel much longer distances. Four powerful engines gave it a top speed of 350 miles an hour, and it was very luxurious for the time. As well as tables and comfortable armchairs for the passengers, and a kitchen for preparing meals, it had a small 'powder room' where lady passengers could put on their make-up before landing.

Britain's intercontinental airline, the British Overseas Aircraft Corporation (BOAC), had ordered twenty-five of the new aircraft for use on its West African routes. In May 1952 one of these was flying from London to Accra in Ghana with eighteen people on board. The journey would take the passengers and crew across the vast expanse of the Sahara, Africa's largest desert.

The pilot, Captain Robert Langley, was a highly experienced airman and had been awarded the Distinguished Flying Cross after completing thirty-six successful missions during his time in the Royal Air Force. This particular journey was one he had already completed eighteen times, and on this occasion he was aided by First Officer Ted Haslam, another former RAF pilot with more than 5,000 hours' flying experience.

Despite their expertise, the Hermes somehow wandered off course during the night without the crew noticing. By sunrise it was more than 1,300 miles from where it should have been. This was a very serious error and Captain Langley realised immediately that the Hermes no longer had enough fuel to reach its destination. He sent out an urgent SOS message by radio and his chief steward, Len Smee, began preparing the passengers for a crash landing.

The Hermes no longer had enough fuel to reach its destination

Not long afterwards, at 8.45 that morning, the fuel tanks ran dry and all four propellers stopped turning. Captain Langley used the wing flaps to slow the Hermes down as much as he could and then warned the passengers that they were beginning to go down. He decided to attempt what's called a belly landing, believing that this would be safer than attempting to use the aircraft's wheels on the soft sand of the Sahara.

This was probably the right decision, but there was a loud bang when the Hermes hit the ground. It took several hundred metres to slide to a halt, and one engine was torn off when the left- or port-wing hit a dune. Luckily, the fuselage of the Hermes remained largely intact and inside the cabin the passengers were stunned but mostly OK. Len's advice had almost certainly saved their lives. Only one person was seriously injured, and that was Ted Haslam, who banged his head on part of the cockpit.

With no fuel left there was little danger of the Hermes catching fire or exploding, but as they clambered from the wreckage the passengers and crew knew they were in deep trouble. They had survived the crash, but how would they get out of the desert?

They had survived the crash, but how would they get out of the desert?

Spread over more than three and a half million square miles, this huge expanse of rock and sand occupies more land than the whole of China or the USA. (Only the desolate, frozen wastes of Antarctica and the Arctic are larger.) In summer the temperature soars to almost 50° Celsius, making the ground too hot walk on, and in parts of the vast, burning desert no rainfall has ever been recorded.

There were supplies of food and water on the ill-fated airliner, but even with these it is hard to survive for very long in such an inhospitable place. No one could say how many hours or even days it would take for a rescue party to reach them. No one knew their precise location and there were particular fears for the health of a six-month-old baby who was travelling on the flight with his mother, Enid Gurney.

Captain Langley was confident that the authorities would have started looking for them as soon as they heard his radio message. In fact, BOAC had already asked an American army helicopter to begin the search from its base in Libya. Unfortunately helicopters are relatively slow and can't cover long distances, but a French military plane had also joined in and was now combing the sand-covered wilderness looking for the crash site.

The crew of the Hermes realised they would be hard to spot from the air, but one of them had an idea. Trevor De Nett climbed back into the wreckage and pulled a mirror off the wall in the ladies' powder room. He knew he could use this to signal to anyone flying overhead, by angling the glass to catch the sun and reflecting it back up into the sky.

As the day wore on the sun rose higher and higher, and the desert became blisteringly hot. It was the French who spotted the wreckage first, although this took several hours. Even then, their Junkers transport plane couldn't land anywhere near the crashed Hermes. Instead several soldiers of the army's French Foreign Legion parachuted down to the desert as their plane slowly circled the site.

Several soldiers of the army's French Foreign Legion parachuted down to the desert

Before flying off again the French pilot dropped some supplies down to the survivors, but there was still no firm plan about how to transport them to safety. Luckily one of the French soldiers was a medical officer, Colonel Lartigau. He bandaged Ted's head and treated the rest of the survivors for minor cuts and bruises. Next, having correctly identified the group's location, he arranged for more Foreign Legion soldiers to drive out into the desert. Atar, the nearest town, was more than eighty miles away, but he hoped they could use their four-wheel-drive vehicles to get the crew and passengers back to civilisation.

Unfortunately this wasn't possible. The nearest the vehicles could get to the group was Hassi el Motleh, an oasis about fifteen miles away. Even with specialised vehicles it took them nearly four full days to reach the oasis, by which time the survivors were sick with sunstroke and exhaustion. Much weakened by their ordeal, they must have been horrified when Colonel Lartigau announced that the only way to save them was for the whole group to make its way on foot to the oasis. Baby Robert would have to be carried the entire way, and the injured Ted Haslam clearly needed to be supported.

It took them nearly four full days to reach the oasis

Crossing the desert in the heat of the day was out of the question so it was decided to make the fifteen-hour trek to Hassi el Motleh after dark. But even at night it was a difficult journey and after being caught in a blinding sandstorm some of the walkers began to think they would never reach the oasis. After a few miles, Captain Langley could tell they had had enough. He called a halt. As the exhausted group slumped to the ground, Len Smee found the energy to go on alone. After several hours, he reached Hassi el Motleh with details about the survivors' whereabouts.

Once again Len had probably saved all their lives. Guided by Len, a second group of soldiers set off from the oasis to look for the stranded passengers. With help from this second group, the survivors eventually made it to the oasis where they were helped on to the rescue vehicles and driven to safety. Sadly Ted didn't make it. Everyone else on Flight 251 was safe, but the co-pilot's injuries were made worse by the heat and the strain of crossing the desert. He died when they reached the oasis and was buried in the sand.

MV *MAERSK ALABAMA*
A modern, American pirate rescue
(Indian Ocean, 2009)

When we think of pirates we usually conjure up images of parrots, wooden legs and colourful, cutlass-wielding adventurers who raid galleons for gold, but piracy still poses a real danger to sailors in many parts of the world. Hundreds of vessels are attacked by pirates every year, ranging from little sailing boats to huge oil tankers and cargo carriers.

In recent years the most dangerous waters have been in the Indian Ocean, especially off the coast of Somalia. Although not all of the attacks are successful, pirate gangs occasionally try to steal the cargo, but usually just kidnap the crew. They threaten to kill all the sailors unless the ship's owner pays a large sum of money to get his vessel back. Sometimes the kidnappers demand several million dollars, and often they get it.

In 2009 a group of Somali pirates captured a fishing boat called the *Win Far 161*. There were only four of them, but they were well armed and very dangerous. After locking up the Taiwanese crew they used the vessel as a base from which to attack a much larger ship called the MV *Maersk Alabama*. This was sailing approximately 240 miles off the coast of Somalia and carrying thousands of tonnes of cargo. Much of it was medical and food aid for the victims of Somalia's long and vicious civil war.

Modern container ships are large but efficient, which means they need only small crews to operate them. The *Maersk Alabama* was enormous, more than 150 metres from end to end, but it had only twenty-three sailors on board when it came under attack. It had been targeted several times before, but this time the pirates were more successful. After several hours of fighting most of the crew locked themselves in the engine room for safety. The pirates' ringleader had been wounded and tied up, but Captain Richard Phillips had been captured by the other three pirates and was being held prisoner.

The crew could prevent the pirates stealing the ship by blocking the controls, but they couldn't stay in the engine room forever. It was hot and uncomfortable down there so they offered the pirates a deal. The crew agreed to hand over their prisoner and some money in exchange for the captain. Because the pirates' own boat had been sunk in the fighting the Somalis then planned to use a lifeboat from the *Maersk Alabama* to get away.

Unfortunately the exchange went wrong because the pirates refused to honour their side of the agreement. Their leader was untied and set free by the crew, but when Captain Phillips showed the pirates how to work the engine in the lifeboat, they kidnapped him again and escaped with him as a hostage.

The pirates refused to honour their side of the agreement

The alarm was raised by the crew and two US navy warships immediately headed for the area. By the following morning the USS *Bainbridge* and the USS *Halyburton* had caught up with the lifeboat containing the pirates and Captain Phillips. The captains of both vessels were careful not to go too close. Staying out of range of the pirates' powerful assault rifles, one of them arranged for an aircraft to drop a mobile phone and a radio down to the lifeboat. This way the navy could talk to the pirates and get reassurance that their hostage was all right.

After two days it was looking like a stand-off or a stalemate. The pirates refused to surrender and the warships couldn't attack them without risking the captain's life. The navy also knew that four more vessels had been captured and were now sailing into the area to help the pirates. If Captain Phillips wasn't rescued before these other pirates arrived, the situation would become even more dangerous.

On the fourth day the leader of the pirates agreed to come on board the *Bainbridge* to have his wounds treated. The other three refused to leave the lifeboat or to release their hostage unless they were paid $2 million. No one wanted to pay the money and, while the navy waited anxiously, the sound of gunshots came from the captured vessel. It seemed as though Captain Phillips had attempted to escape on his own, but he'd been recaptured while trying to swim away. After beating him up, the pirates then threw the telephone and the radio into the sea to show they weren't prepared to negotiate any further.

However, things were about to change. Without being seen by the pirates, a team of highly trained US navy SEALs had parachuted down into the water and found a hiding place on board the *Halyburton*. These commandos are called SEALs because they are trained and equipped to fight in hazardous operations in all environments – sea, air and land.

Much like the soldiers of the British SAS, everyone recruited by the SEALs is taught many special skills, including the sort of accurate long-range marksmanship needed to work as snipers. A sniper is a person who uses a high-powered rifle and telescopic sights to spot and shoot an enemy who may be hundreds of metres away. The record for a successful hit is more than two miles, and many of America's finest military snipers are navy SEALs.

team of highly trained US navy SEALs had parachuted down into the water

The SEALs had been keeping a close eye on what was going on in the lifeboat and could see that the pirates were getting more and more nervous. Sophisticated night-vision equipment was brought out when it got dark and, when one of the SEALs thought he saw a pirate point his gun at the captain's back, the order was given to attack the lifeboat immediately. Within seconds all three pirates were dead, shot by three SEALs who now boarded the lifeboat to untie Captain Phillips.

The whole incident had lasted five days, but the captain was safe. The leader of the pirates was flown back to America eventually – the only survivor – and was jailed for thirty-three years. Later it was revealed that the *Maersk Alabama* was the first American ship to be captured by pirates in nearly 200 years, and that the US navy SEALs had been acting under the orders of the president, Barack Obama, when they shot the three men.

SHAVARSH KARAPETYAN
A champion swimmer dives after a bus (Armenia, 1976)

Two brothers were out on a twelve-mile training run one September evening when they heard the noise of a bus crashing into a concrete barrier, followed by a loud splash. The bus had accidentally driven off a dam which formed part of a large reservoir near Yerevan, the capital of Armenia. By the time the runners, Shavarsh and Kamo Karapetyan, got close enough to see what had happened, the bus was at least twenty-five metres from the shore and lying under ten metres of chilly water.

The bus was at least twenty-five metres from the shore and lying under ten metres of chilly water

The vehicle was an old-fashioned trolleybus, a type of bus fitted with long metal poles on the roof which were used to collect electricity from overhead wires to power its motor. This particular trolleybus was crowded that evening, carrying a mix of factory workers, housewives and children, some of whom were knocked unconscious when it suddenly veered sharply to the right and nosedived off the dam.

Standing on the dam, the brothers could see bubbles rising from the spot where the bus had disappeared. This meant that there was air inside for the passengers to breathe, but they knew it would soon run out.

Both of them immediately dived into the water. The sinking bus had disturbed the mud at the bottom of the reservoir, which meant they couldn't see much. Instead they had to use the poles on the roof to guide them down to the bottom of the reservoir. At such a depth it was hard to know what they could do, and as their breath began to run out both men shot back up to the surface.

They were both expert swimmers and the run around the reservoir was one they did regularly. It formed part of a tough training regime which had helped Shavarsh to break several world records. He had also won eight gold medals in various European championships. His sport was finswimming, an activity which requires great strength and stamina, as well as special breathing techniques. To get as fit as possible, Shavarsh used to run huge distances every day of the week, often with a twenty-kilogram bag of sand strapped to his back.

The water was freezing cold, but Shavarsh was determined to have a go at rescuing the passengers from the trolleybus. He didn't know how many people were trapped in there but he could see that none of them were managing to get out on their own. As he and his younger brother were such strong swimmers he felt they should do whatever they could to help. Shavarsh told his brother to stay on the surface where they were treading water. That way Kamo would be able to help any rescued passengers back to the shore.

Shavarsh dived down again, but it was still hard to see much, so he felt his way along the side of the bus. He was hoping he could find an open door or an open window. He couldn't find either though, and when he did reach the door it must have been jammed because he couldn't open it from the outside. He began kicking hard at one of the windows to try and force his way in. This wasn't easy either, not this far underwater, where the pressure must have made his movements look a bit like he was dancing in slow motion.

He began kicking hard at one of the windows to try and force his way in

Eventually, using a sort of karate kick, Shavarsh was able to break one of the large windows at the back of the bus. He cut his leg badly on the jagged glass and then his arms as well as he reached inside to force the window out of its frame. He didn't let the pain stop him, though: feeling around in the dark, he began to pull the first few passengers out before sending them up to his brother on the surface.

Holding his breath and working as fast as he could, Shavarsh knew he wouldn't be able to get everyone out. The poor visibility meant it was hard to tell if he was pulling out live passengers or dead bodies. He realised his best hope was just to pull as many people as possible through the broken window. Every time he felt an arm or a leg, he yanked at it until he was clear of the bus.

Every time he felt an arm or a leg, he yanked at it until he was clear of the bus

Fortunately by now a few of the other passengers were managing to find their own way out the same way.

Each time he hauled someone up to the surface, Shavarsh took five deep breaths before diving back down again. Kamo was kept busy helping everyone to the shore. Like Shavarsh he was working too fast to tell who was alive and who was dead. He too realised that the most important thing was to keep working as fast as possible.

Soon other people started arriving to offer help. Some of them had small boats, which they used to help Kamo get the victims out of the water. Others waited on the shore where they tried to treat any injured passengers and revive those who were brought up unconscious.

After a quarter of an hour or so, Shavarsh was still diving, but the onlookers could see that he was beginning to tire and began calling him to stop. Reluctantly Shaversh realised that they were right. He didn't want to stop, but none of the passengers could survive this long underwater so there was no point in putting himself in any further danger.

In the rush and panic neither of the brothers had even tried to keep count of the number of people they had pulled out of the water. However, it is

now known that between them the pair managed to save at least twenty of the passengers. There had been more than ninety people on the trolleybus before the crash, but sadly about half of them had drowned. It was a tragedy for the local community, but no one at the scene was in any doubt that without Shavarsh and Kamo the number of victims would have been much higher.

Between them the pair managed to save at least twenty of the passengers

Unfortunately, the strain of repeatedly diving down to the bus took its toll on this fit young swimming champion. At home later that evening he collapsed with a fever, brought on by the cold and by the polluted water of the reservoir. He was also completely exhausted, and ended up being hospitalised for almost a month.

Eventually he was able to return to his training and to international swimming competitions, but it was never quite the same. The truth was that, after the trauma of the crash and his brave rescue effort, Shavarsh Karapetyan found he didn't like being in the water any more. He wasn't scared of it, but he hated it. He went on to win a few more medals, proving to himself and to others that he could still do it, but at just twenty-three years old the world's fastest underwater swimmer had had enough and he retired from the sport.

PASANG TENZING
History's highest-ever mountain rescue (Nepal, 2013)

The tallest mountain in the world may not be the toughest one to climb, but at 8,848 metres (nearly five and a half miles) its icy summit makes Everest an irresistible target for many of the world's top climbers.

More than 4,000 people have climbed to the 'roof of the world' since Sir Edmund Hilary and Tenzing Norgay first conquered Everest in 1953, but nearly three hundred have died trying. This makes it one of the most dangerous places on the planet, but amazingly it's nowhere near the worst. Other peaks in central Asia have even higher fatality rates, although the current holder of this deadly record, Annapurna, is only the tenth tallest mountain in the world.

It's not just exposure to the cold that kills climbers high up in the Himalayas, but also exhaustion and altitude sickness caused by the dangerously thin atmosphere. On Everest nearly seventy mountaineers have been killed by ice falls and earthquakes, and in avalanches, just one of which caused nineteen deaths in 2015.

On a clear day the view from the top is certainly spectacular, but the best climbers know that even if you manage to reach the summit you're still only halfway home. People die on the way down as well as on the way up, and so the sensible place to celebrate a successful climb is at the bottom of Mount Everest, not at the top.

Even now only one person has ever made it back from the summit of Everest after a solo expedition

Almost no one climbs it alone, and even now only one person has ever made it back from the summit of Everest after a solo expedition. Instead mountaineers tend to work in teams, and even the most expert ones use professional guides from the local Sherpa community.

The Sherpas have lived in the mountains of Nepal for centuries and they call Mount Everest *Chomolungma*, which means 'Mother of the World'. With their huge experience and a deep knowledge of the Himalayas, many of them are outstanding climbers. Tenzing Norgay was the first Sherpa ever to climb Everest, and three-quarters of a century later the record for the greatest number of successful ascents is held by three more Sherpas, each of whom has reached the summit an incredible twenty-one times. Everest's most successful female mountaineer is also a Sherpa, and so is its fastest.

In 2004 Pemba Dorje slashed the time taken for a round trip when he managed to climb to the summit and back again in just eight hours and ten minutes. Almost exactly a year earlier yet another Sherpa had become the youngest person ever to reach the summit.

Everest's most successful female mountaineer is also a Sherpa

(Fifteen-year-old Ming Kipa has since lost her title to a thirteen-year-old.) And in 2005 another Sherpa and his Nepalese girlfriend became the first people to get married at the top of the world's highest mountain.

Because Sherpas like these are the real Everest experts, it is perhaps not surprising that they have been involved in many of the most dangerous and most daring rescues in modern mountaineering history. Sometimes they have saved lives while accompanying climbers who have become sick or injured. But often Sherpas have gone out of their way to help some of the hundreds of tourists who come to their country each year in the hope of pitting themselves against Mother Nature and the mountains.

Pasang Tenzing and his six brothers have reached the summit more than fifty times between them, so by 2013 he was already a very well-known face on Everest. In May of that year Pasang was involved in the rescue of an injured Nepali-Canadian climber who had got into severe difficulties on his way down from the top.

The mountaineer had become stranded somewhere above 8,500 metres. This is well inside what climbers call 'the death zone' – the most dangerous part of the mountain. It is also far beyond the safe operating altitude of a normal rescue helicopter. A few years earlier a Frenchman called Didier Delsalle managed to land a special high-performance Eurocopter right on the summit, but at this sort of height the Himalayan air is dangerously thin. No matter how skilled the pilot, a helicopter's turbine engines can't function properly without sufficient oxygen, and its rotor blades struggle to get the necessary 'lift' to fly reliably and safely.

At this sort of height the Himalayan air is dangerously thin

Because of this, Pasang and his Sherpa colleagues realised that they needed to get the injured climber further down the mountain to give him any chance of survival. He couldn't possibly climb down himself so they would have to carry him. They began their descent around lunchtime and it took until 8 p.m. before the group had reached the relative safety of an area called South Col Camp. By then it was much too late to go on so they decided to stop for the night.

At 7,950 metres, the camp was still situated too high up for a safe helicopter evacuation so the following morning the Sherpas continued their descent. Doing this was awkward and very dangerous, and their progress was painfully slow. It took several more hours to lower the casualty just a couple of hundred metres over very difficult ground. The Sherpas were heading for a place where a helicopter rescue might be possible. Pasang knew that even if they reached it there still wouldn't be anywhere to land an aircraft. No one had ever successfully carried out such a complex and difficult rescue at this height before.

The pilot chosen for the job was an Italian called Maurizio Folini. To make the helicopter as light as possible, his team removed everything they could, including the seats and even the doors.

Because he wouldn't be able to land anywhere near the casualty, Maurizio was going to attempt a perilous life-saving manoeuvre called a helicopter emergency longline last option (or HELLO). It's called the last option because it involves so much risk that it is never, ever used unless there is no possible alternative.

In a HELLO rescue a strong cable is lowered down to the ground from the helicopter and then used to winch the injured climber back up. It's a very difficult thing to get right, even in good weather on flat ground, and it normally requires a second crew member to be lowered down with the cable to help the casualty. This time though, because he had to save weight, Maurizio was going to fly up Everest on his own.

Doing it this way put even more of the risk on to Pasang. He was now responsible not just for getting the injured climber to the right place at the right time, but also for getting him secured on to the cable. It would also be Pasang's job to get the patient into the helicopter as it hovered twenty metres overhead.

Maurizio was going to fly up Everest on his own

Incredibly, he managed this tricky manoeuvre without incident. Unfortunately the need to save weight meant that Pasang couldn't stay in the helicopter himself. Instead, having already climbed to the summit of Everest, and then carried a dying climber out of the death zone, he and the other Sherpas had to climb all the way down to the bottom again. Happily they made it, and Pasang Tenzing is still working on Everest as one of its best and most famous mountain guides.

SS *SUEVIC*
The vicar and the volunteers
(England, 1907)

For nearly 200 years sailors in trouble around the coast of Britain have relied on crews of unpaid volunteers to get them out of danger. Men and women of the Royal National Lifeboat Institution (RNLI) have saved literally thousands of lives in that time, and more than 600 of them have died trying.

The RNLI's distinctive blue and orange lifeboats are launched in even the worst storms, and the people they rescue include professional mariners and amateur sailors, as well as numerous holidaymakers and hikers cut off by the incoming tide.

It's hard to say which rescue was the most dangerous in all that time – there have been too many of them – but one of the most amazing took place more than a hundred years ago. The rescue of a badly damaged ocean liner off the wild, treacherous coast of Cornwall involved no fewer than four different lifeboat crews. Not a single life was lost during the overnight operation, and well over 500 people were brought to safety.

The SS *Suevic* was a 12,000-tonne steamship owned by the same company as the *Titanic*. One dark night in March 1907 nearly 400 passengers and 141 crew were sailing from Australia to England when the ship ran into thick fog. The crew had completed this journey several times over the previous six years, but this time the captain made a bad navigational error. About a quarter of a mile out to sea the *Suevic* hit a dangerous ridge of submerged rocks and began to flood. When it proved impossible to get the ship off the ridge, the captain gave the order for red distress flares to be fired into the air and the passengers got ready to evacuate the ship.

The bright flares lit up the night sky and were seen by many people living in villages along the coast. They alerted the crews of four local lifeboat stations, and sixty volunteers from Porthleven, the Lizard, Cadgwith and Coverack put to sea as fast as they could.

The bright flares lit up the night sky

In those days lifeboatmen used simple wooden rowing boats. These were less than twelve metres in length and, lacking any kind of an engine, they were propelled using six sets of oars. Before the boats could set out for the *Suevic*, they had to be dragged across the beach by hand. Each carried

a crew of fifteen dressed in waterproof oilskins and bulky, uncomfortable cork lifejackets in case anyone fell overboard.

A strong south-westerly gale was blowing, and some of the crews had to row several miles just to find the ship. In the thick fog the visibility was so poor that although they could hear the *Suevic*'s horn above the storm they couldn't actually see it. As a result, the first crew didn't know they had reached the right place until their boat crashed against the liner's steel hull, throwing one of them into the water.

Before the boats could set out for the *Suevic*, they had to be dragged across the beach by hand

Getting this far had demanded a huge effort from the men, who had to row as fast as they could against heavy seas and directly into the wind. Also they would have known that, with so many passengers and crew on board the stranded vessel, the terrifying trip out and back in the storm was one they would have to do many times before the night was out.

Even then, reaching the *Suevic* was just the first stage of the rescue. Transferring the passengers from ship to boat in such a rough sea was even more hazardous, especially as more than seventy of them were babies and small children who needed carrying as they cried out for their mothers. Back on the beach, in complete darkness, dozens of village women waded through the waves to help bring the boats in. Often standing up to their waists in the cold water, they hoisted the children out of the wooden boats and carried them to safety.

Most lifeboatmen were ordinary fishermen and farmers, but among those who risked their lives that night was Harry Vyvyan. As the vicar of

Cadgwith he knew his local crew well although he never went to sea with them. This time was different though. This was no ordinary rescue and, determined to help, he jumped into the boat. When it reached the *Suevic* he quickly climbed into one of the ship's own lifeboats and did what he could to bring it back to shore full of passengers.

Harry's plan was to take the boat out again to the liner as soon as the first group of women and children had been safely landed on the beach. Unfortunately his boat was badly damaged before it could make the return trip. After being tossed around by the waves, it was smashed to pieces on the rocks. Harry refused to be beaten and, ignoring the obvious dangers, leapt into the sea and started swimming back to shore to get another vessel.

Harry refused to be beaten

On the beach at Polpeor Cove bonfires were lit to provide some warmth and comfort for the rescued passengers, but for the vicar and the volunteers there was no chance to rest. For the next sixteen hours the crews rowed out to the *Suevic* and back again, helping survivors into the lifeboats and depositing them on the beach. They were cold, wet, scared and bedraggled, but safe.

In all, the lifeboat crews managed to rescue an amazing 456 people. The remaining crew and passengers were taken off the ship by three tugboats, which had steamed down the coast to help and, despite the appalling weather, not a single person had died. At the time it was by far the RNLI's largest-ever rescue, and more than a hundred years later it still is.

Apollo 13

'Houston, we've had a problem'
(Outer Space, 1970)

More than five hundred people from nearly forty countries have travelled out to space in a rocket, but only twelve people have ever walked on the Moon. They did this as part of America's Apollo programme, which launched seven manned missions to the Moon in the 1960s and 1970s. Six of the crews made it there and back, but the rescue of the seventh is a remarkable story of heroism, teamwork and incredible ingenuity.

The astronauts flew to the Moon in Saturn V rockets, the tallest, heaviest and most powerful rockets ever launched. These were also the most expensive and most complicated machines ever built, and among the fastest with a top speed of around 24,000 miles an hour. Each one had three million components so there was plenty that could go wrong. As the Saturn V also carried thousands of tonnes of highly explosive fuel, enough to travel a million miles, even the tiniest malfunction could have caused a complete disaster.

The first few launches went according to plan, but a couple of days after Apollo 13 blasted off from the launch pad at Florida's Cape Canaveral in April 1970 the three-man crew heard a loud bang. When one of the astronauts looked out of the window he could see a jet of gas shooting out of the back of the spacecraft. This was the crew's oxygen supply disappearing into space, and there was nothing he could do to stop it. One of those tiny malfunctions had occurred and it looked like it was going to turn into a disaster.

He could see a jet of gas shooting out of the back of the spacecraft

At the time of the explosion, Commander Jim Lovell, Jack Swigert and Fred Haise were nearly 200,000 miles from home. It was obvious at once that they wouldn't be able to land on the Moon now, but they weren't at all sure they would be able to make it back to Earth either. Every manned spacecraft needs adequate supplies of oxygen, not just for the crew to breathe but because it is used to make water and to generate electricity (using a device called a fuel cell).

Commander Lovell sent an urgent radio message to Mission Control at Houston in Texas explaining that they'd had a problem. He sounded calm, and so did the flight controllers when they responded, but it was clear to everyone that the crew was in trouble. No one knew what had caused the problem. It was too late to fix it – the oxygen was all gone – and no one had any idea about how to rescue the crew.

Although a Saturn V rocket is 110 metres long and weighs 2,800 tonnes, only a tiny part of it is used by the crew to return to Earth. This little capsule is called the Command Module and it's not much bigger than a garden shed. Another small part, the Lunar Module, is designed to land on the Moon. The rest is left to drift through space before eventually crashing down into the sea.

The crew knew they needed to preserve as much as possible of the capsule's air and power if they were to have any chance at all of a safe return. To help with this they decided to climb through a hatch into the Lunar Module. By using this as a sort of lifeboat they could preserve what oxygen they had left and save their reserves of electrical power while the flight controllers worked out what to do next.

They decided to climb through a hatch into the Lunar Module

There were several problems with this plan. The capsule was cramped inside but it was designed to carry three astronauts. The Lunar Module was designed to carry only two of them. This is because, during a normal Moon landing, two astronauts use it to go down to the surface while the third stays behind in orbit. This also meant that the Lunar Module was intended to be used for only a day and a half, not four days, which is how long the crew calculated they needed to get back to Earth.

An incredible 400,000 men and women were involved in the Apollo programme, and down on the ground hundreds of engineers and mathematicians were now working around the clock trying to find a way to rescue the crew. When the explosion occurred, the spacecraft was still heading away from Earth. Now it was decided that the crew's only hope of survival was to use the rocket's last remaining engine to travel round the Moon and then get back on course for Earth. Nothing like this had ever been tried before, and no one knew whether or not it would work.

When the explosion occurred, the spacecraft was still heading away from Earth

Back on Earth the job of the engineers and mathematicians was to calculate precisely how and when to fire the little rocket to give the astronauts the best possible chance of getting back. The maths involved was incredibly complex and even the tiniest calculation had to be done with 100 per cent accuracy. Everyone knew they had only one opportunity to get it right. If they got it wrong the rocket would have no more fuel left for a second attempt.

For several days and nights no one went home or managed to get more than a few minutes' sleep. When they did take a break they lay down on the floor beneath their desks. Meanwhile, hundreds of thousands of miles away, in the darkness of space, conditions for the three astronauts were even more uncomfortable.

With the rocket's main computer switched off to save power, it quickly got damp and extremely cold inside the 'lifeboat'. The astronauts felt they could cope with the discomfort, but with three of them instead of two they were using up much more oxygen than the Lunar Module was designed for.

Before long, their air supply began to turn poisonous as the level of deadly carbon dioxide rose higher and higher.

The air inside continued to get more and more poisonous

Normally, to stop this happening, astronauts use a type of filter device called a scrubber. Mission Control sent the astronauts a message saying there were some scrubbers in the capsule which could be used to solve the problem. Unfortunately they were square, not circular, which meant they wouldn't fit in the Lunar Module, so the air inside continued to get more and more poisonous.

If something wasn't done quickly the crew would die, but luckily someone had an idea. A team of engineers on the ground started experimenting with various pieces of equipment. Using only the same items the astronauts had on board the spacecraft, and working as fast as possible, they had to devise a way to make the square scrubbers fit the circular fixtures in the Lunar Module. If they could solve this problem it might enable the astronauts to breathe the air inside for a little bit longer.

Eventually they found a way to do this. As quickly as they could they explained to the crew how they had used socks, plastic bags and some ordinary sticky tape to modify the scrubbers. The crew tried doing the same thing and it worked! The result looked messy, and they knew it wouldn't last for long, but it was a brilliant solution which kept the air supply safe for a little while longer.

After this it still took several more hours to calculate when to fire the last remaining rocket, and for how long. The tension was growing unbearable, and three lives hung in the balance, but finally the rocket was fired. Apollo 13 slowly turned and began moving in the right direction.

Eventually the men returned to their capsule and, after separating from the damaged rocket section, they re-entered the Earth's atmosphere in the normal way. Even then no one could be sure they would survive. The capsule's parachutes might have been damaged in the explosion, and without them to slow it down the capsule would be destroyed as it hit the surface of the Pacific Ocean.

During re-entry, radio contact with the crew is always lost for several minutes. Observers on the ground can only look out for the tiny capsule and keep their fingers crossed that everything will be OK. After a few tense minutes someone spotted it high above the ocean. Seconds later its three red and white parachutes were seen to open as normal, and shortly afterwards the capsule splashed down into the sea.

After a few tense minutes someone spotted the capsule high above the ocean

After nearly six days in space, the crew was safe. Jim, Jack and Fred may not have reached the Moon, but they had survived against seemingly impossible odds. A combination of teamwork, ingenuity and raw courage had brought them back home, and nearly fifty years later these three men still hold the record for travelling further away from Earth than anyone in history: 248,655 miles – and back again.

The Seabees
Saving a family teetering on the edge (USA, 2012)

After colliding with a BMW on a tall bridge outside Buellton in California, a heavy, eighteen-wheeled truck plunged more than twenty metres down into a ravine and exploded on impact. The driver was killed instantly, and the car he had hit was left dangling from the bridge high above the burning wreck.

A teacher and her two young daughters were trapped inside the car, but help arrived almost immediately. The police and fire brigade were on site within minutes and got ready to cut them out of the badly mangled car so they could be taken to hospital.

The car was so badly damaged that it was hard to tell whether it was a saloon or a hatchback. The police later said it was amazing that the occupants hadn't been killed by the impact. They could see through the broken windows that Kelli Groves and at least one of her children had been injured in the crash. The baby looked like she had been saved by her car seat, but they had something much more urgent to worry about than her injured mother and sister.

The Nojoqui Creek Bridge is really two separate bridges, one heading north and the other south along Highway 101. Between the two is a large gap. After being hit from behind, the dark-coloured BMW had smashed through the concrete barrier on one side of the bridge. It was now hanging perilously over the gap.

The wreckage looked dangerously unstable. The rescuers were worried that if the car shifted only a centimetre or two it could become completely unbalanced. If that happened it would follow the truck over the edge of the bridge. Similarly, if anyone climbed on to the car and tried to get the family out, the extra weight could be enough to send it down into the ravine along with Kelli, ten-year-old Sage and baby Mylo.

If the car shifted only a centimetre or two it could become completely unbalanced

While the police and fire crews wondered what they should do next, a passing tow-truck driver offered his help. He said he could attach his cables to the car and this might stop it falling down on to the burning truck. He knew the cables on his tow truck hadn't been designed for this sort of thing, and it was possible that they weren't strong enough. But even if they were, the BMW would still be in the wrong position for the firefighters to begin using their cutting equipment to get the family out.

As Kelli tried to keep her daughters from panicking, a small group of US navy personnel ran on to the bridge. Six of them had been driving some military equipment back to their base at Port Hueneme, about eighty miles away. They'd stopped after seeing the cloud of black smoke from the burning truck and wanted to know if they could help. The first job they were given was to clear the long queue of traffic heading north, which they did by directing the vehicles away from the scene of the crash.

Kelli tried to keep her daughters from panicking

The group were Seabees, a nickname given to the men and women of the United States Naval Construction Battalions (or CBs). Normally their work involves building airfields and runways, military hospitals, camps and bomb-proof bunkers, but like other navy sailors the Seabees also fight when America goes to war.

While the Seabees tried to keep the traffic moving, the firefighters got out a piece of cutting equipment known as the 'jaws of life', which looks like a giant pair of powerful scissors. It's used to cut through the steel body of a crashed car when it is not possible to get the occupants out the normal way using the doors.

Unfortunately they still couldn't see how they could use the device on the car without risking the lives of those inside. What they really needed was something to hold the BMW in place while they worked to free Kelli and her children. Hearing them discussing this idea, one of the Seabees mentioned that his unit had some equipment which might be useful.

The machines the Seabees were taking back to Port Hueneme included a vehicle called a telescopic handler. This looks like a cross between a forklift truck and a small crane and it has an extendable steel boom or arm. The arm is used to pick up heavy loads and carry them around naval yards and building sites. If the boom on this one was long enough to reach across the three-metre gap between the two bridges, it could be used to support the BMW while the firefighters worked to lift Kelli and her daughters out of the wreckage.

The handler was stuck in traffic about a hundred metres back down the road where the Seabees had abandoned it after realising their journey to Port Hueneme was going to be delayed. One of its operators was Petty Officer Michael McCracken and he ran back to get it after describing his plan to the police and firefighters.

Climbing into the driving seat of the handler it took Michael a few moments to get it out of the traffic. Once he had done this he drove back towards the scene of the accident and steered his vehicle into position on the south-bound section of the bridge. Before long he had parked directly opposite the spot where Kelli's car had crashed through the barrier.

With the handler facing the firefighters on the other side of the bridge, Michael and the other Seabees extended the steel boom across the gap between the two roadways. It was just long enough to span the gap. Very carefully, they manoeuvred the twin forks at the far end of the arm so that these sat directly beneath the wrecked car.

Michael and the other Seabees extended the steel boom across the gap

It was a very delicate operation. If the pointed steel forks hit the car they could cause more injuries to the occupants. If the car moved even slightly it could topple down on to the truck, killing everyone inside. There was also a risk that, with such a heavy load at the end of the forks, the handler might tip over on the other side of the bridge.

It took a while to get the forks into position, but when the Seabees were confident that they had managed to stabilise the car,

They began slicing through its metal body with the jaws

the firefighters climbed over the barrier and on to the wreckage of the BMW. Moving carefully over the roof they began slicing through its metal body with the jaws. It must have been a tense few moments as everyone listened to the noise of the jaws doing their work.

Eventually the firefighters managed to cut a large hole in the body of the car and began the careful task of lifting the girls and their mother out. Mylo emerged unscathed – her seat had saved her, and she had slept through much of the drama. Kelli and Sage were not so lucky, but they were soon out of the car and were taken to hospital in a helicopter which had been standing by. After a week or so, they were allowed home to begin the process of recovering from what could have been an even more horrifying accident.

THE SAN JOSÉ MINE
Sixty-nine days in the dark
(Chile, 2010)

When a shaft in a gold mine collapsed, trapping thirty-three miners more than 700 metres underground, it was a shock but hardly a surprise.

Mining can be a well-paid job in South America but only because it is hard work and extremely dangerous. Mining accidents are not at all unusual and the San José mine has certainly had its fair share of them in the past.

Rock-falls and collapses at the mine had already claimed the lives of eight miners and injured others. In 2007 it was ordered to be closed when a geologist was killed, and when it reopened three years later another miner called Gino Cortés lost one of his legs.

The worst accident at the mine occurred just a few weeks after this, when a large rock-fall completely blocked the entrance tunnel. A number of miners managed to scramble to safety, but dozens more were still missing when the dust finally cleared from the air.

The mine is in a very remote part of the country and lies hundreds of metres beneath the Atacama Desert. This covers more than 40,000 square miles and is a largely empty wasteland of rock and lava. It's one of the driest places on Earth (almost no one lives there) and it is sometimes used by film companies looking for locations they can use for scenes set on Mars.

Thirty-three men were reported to be missing, but no one knew whether they were dead or alive. In fact, for several days no one even knew where they were. The mine is an extremely old one (it opened in the 1880s) and many of the maps showing the layout of its tunnels and shafts were wrong or out of date.

Thirty-three men were reported to be missing, but no one knew whether they were dead or alive

Miners on the surface spent two days trying to clear the entrance in an attempt to free the trapped men, but each time they found their path blocked by more fallen rocks. After a second rock-fall they gave up and heavy machinery was brought in to dig a new entrance at one of the mine's narrow ventilation shafts. Work soon stopped on this too, though, as there were fears that vibrations from the equipment would cause another catastrophic collapse.

Rescuers now started drilling boreholes down into the rock. These were designed to be even narrower than a ventilation shaft so they took less time to drill. Each one was only fourteen centimetres wide, far too narrow for anyone to crawl through, but everyone hoped that they would help find where the miners were – and if they were still alive.

Even drilling these narrow boreholes took time, and after the first few there was still no good news. In the end it took seventeen days and eight different attempts before the miners were finally located. The eighth borehole was drilled through nearly 700 metres of solid rock to a point about three miles from the mine entrance. When the drill came back up, the men operating it found a note taped to the end of it. Written on the note in Spanish were the words *Estamos bien en el refugio, los 33* ('We are well in the refuge, the 33').

> When the drill came back up, the men operating it found a note taped to the end of it

By now hundreds of miners' wives, families and friends were waiting nervously at the surface. They were overjoyed at the discovery of the note, but still no one had any idea how the men could be brought out. It was impossible to know if any of them were injured or how well they were coping with their long confinement – but it was a start.

Emergency supplies of food and water were kept down the mine, but there were usually only enough for two or three days. In fact, by carefully rationing these supplies, the miners had been able to make them last two weeks. Now though they had run out, and each of the men is thought to have lost around six kilograms. When a video camera was lowered down the deep hole they could all be seen in the darkness. The men – thirty-two

Chileans and a Bolivian – were dirty and unshaven, and glistening with sweat from the heat of the mine. They seemed in quite good spirits, though, and according to their foreman, Luis Urzúa, they were well organised.

The company which owned the mine didn't have the equipment or the know-how to handle a major rescue effort like this and so the Chilean government sent its own experts to help. Soon they had offers of help from several overseas mining corporations and even a team from NASA, the American space agency.

Around the world a billion people or more switched on their television sets to see the drama unfold

The Chileans insisted they would lead the rescue attempt, but it quickly became an international story. Around the world a billion people or more switched on their television sets to see the drama unfold, and companies from many different countries sent equipment and engineers.

It still wasn't clear how or when the miners would be rescued. While various plans were being discussed and rejected, food and water, medical supplies, clothes and bedding were sent down the narrow borehole to make the men as comfortable as possible. Eventually it was decided to drill three separate escape shafts to give the men the best possible chance of survival. Because the mine is so old there was the risk of another dangerous collapse, but it was hoped that at least one of the shafts would be suitable to get the men out.

Work on the first shaft began on the twenty-fifth day using a huge Australian machine called a raise borer. This had to be driven out to the mine on several trucks and assembled on site. It is normally used to dig circular holes without using explosives, which was important as an explosion could easily cause another rockfall. It would need the exhausted miners to dig out several tonnes of rock at the bottom of the shaft, but in the end this plan ran into technical difficulties and had to be abandoned.

By the time work began on the next shaft the miners had been underground for a month. This second attempt used an American air-core drill to widen one of the boreholes so that it could then be used as an escape shaft. For safety reasons the work had to be done in stages, first enlarging the shaft from fourteen to thirty centimetres, then widening it from thirty to seventy-one. Unfortunately, cutting through the exceptionally hard rock put an incredible strain on the drill, and its specially hardened steel tip was in danger of becoming worn out.

An explosion could easily cause another rockfall

On the forty-fifth day the third rescue attempt began, using a Canadian oil-rig drill. This was even bigger than the raise borer and had so many gigantic components that it took around forty trucks just to get it to the mine. Its immense size and power should have made it the fastest of all the machines, but it too ran into difficulties. The miners were still stuck underground on the fiftieth day, longer than any miner anywhere in the world had ever been trapped before.

The air-core drill seemed to offer the best chance, but it still took sixty-five days before the widened bore hole reached the miners. At last the Chilean minister for mining was able to announce that the final stage of the rescue plan could begin. This new shaft was still very narrow at just seventy-one centimetres, but it now looked possible to bring the miners back up to the surface.

To do this the Chileans planned to use a device they had designed called the Fénix Capsule. With help from NASA, four of these had been constructed by the Chilean navy while the shafts were being excavated.

Each cylindrical capsule looks like a bullet or a torpedo and is just large enough for a man to stand up inside it. As well as an oxygen supply it is fitted with speakers and a microphone so that the occupant can communicate with the rescue team above. Sixteen wheels set into the outer shell of the capsule would help it to move smoothly through the shaft as it is lowered down to the miners and then winched back up with one of them inside.

With only a single shaft completed, only one capsule could be used at a time and only one person could fit inside. It would take around fifteen minutes to lower it down to the men, and bringing it back up would take slightly longer. This meant that, once the necessary safety checks had been carried out, it was still going to be many hours before all the men were brought back to the surface.

To help the weakened miners climb into the capsule, six of their colleagues bravely volunteered to go down the shaft to help. Because the miners had been trapped in the dark for so long, the rescuers took special sunglasses down with them. It was vital that the men carried on wearing these for several days afterwards to avoid the desert sunlight damaging their eyes.

Six of their colleagues bravely volunteered to go down the shaft to help

Working non-stop it took nearly a day and a half to get all the men out of the mine, and during that time one of the volunteers spent more than twenty-five hours down the hole. It had taken them well over two months, but the Chileans had done it: in an industry where deaths and injuries happen all the time, they had managed to rescue all thirty-three of the trapped men.

CHANNING MOSS
A bomb inside a soldier's body (Afghanistan, 2006)

It was a bright sunny day when two dozen American soldiers of the 10th Mountain Division came under attack during a mission in war-torn Afghanistan. The men were travelling in a convoy of Humvees, a type of off-road military vehicle with hardened steel armour plating and bullet-proof glass. This offers good protection against ordinary gunfire, but when one of the vehicles was attacked using rocket propelled grenades the windscreen broke and Private Channing Moss was hit badly in the side of his body.

The rocket-propelled grenade (RPG) is a mini-missile designed to be used against tanks, and it is a ferociously effective weapon. At one end it has a rocket with three or four stabilising fins which help it to be aimed very accurately over a distance of several hundred metres. At the other end is a high-explosive warhead that normally detonates the moment the RPG hits its target.

Although two of the RPGs had caused a lot of damage to the Humvee, the one which hit Channing Moss in the lower body had for some reason failed to explode. It had also failed to kill him, which is extraordinary for a metal object more than a metre long that had been travelling at more than 500 miles per hour when it smashed into the vehicle.

In the heat of battle the twenty-three-year-old soldier didn't realise straight away that he'd been hit. When he looked down Channing could see that his body was actually smoking, but he was in such a state of shock that he probably didn't fully understand what had just happened.

Once it has been fired an RPG can explode at any moment. Because of this the sensible thing was for the other soldiers to get out of the Humvee as quickly as possible and get as far away as they could. They all knew that if it went off it wouldn't just kill Channing but everyone else within ten metres as well. Even so, nobody moved, including Jared Angell, who was sitting next to the injured private and reached for his emergency first aid kit.

> **When he looked down Channing could see that his body was actually smoking**

The other soldiers called Jared 'Doc' because he was the convoy's medic. Doc realised immediately what had happened and ordered Channing to stop looking down. He didn't want his colleague to panic at the sight of his injuries or to change position suddenly. If he moved even slightly, the RPG might explode and kill them all. Even if it didn't explode, any movement could worsen the soldier's injuries.

While one of the other soldiers radioed headquarters to get a medical evacuation helicopter out to them, Doc squeezed Channing's hand to make sure he was still alive. Next he got some bandages out of the first aid kit as he knew he had to stop Channing's bleeding as quickly as possible. Pulling the RPG out would be far too dangerous so he used more bandages to strap the missile in place to prevent it moving around. 'I'm going do everything I can,' he told Channing. 'You keep fighting with me and I'll keep fighting with you.'

The message to headquarters had just said there were wounded soldiers who needed rescuing. It said nothing about one of them having an unexploded bomb inside him because the army has rules about not taking live explosives on to helicopters. Doc knew that the specially equipped Black Hawk helicopter wouldn't be able to land near

He used more bandages to strap the missile in place to prevent it moving around

the Humvee while the fighting was going on and so for fifteen minutes he concentrated on keeping Channing conscious and alive.

Eventually the helicopter was able to land, but the pilot realised immediately that the problem was far more serious than he'd been told. If he took Channing on to the helicopter and the RPG exploded it would kill even more people than if it had blown up inside the Humvee. He had his crew to worry about, as well as three other wounded soldiers who were being loaded on to the Black Hawk.

At the same time it was obvious that Doc couldn't do any more to help Channing, who needed urgent, life-saving surgery in a properly equipped emergency hospital. Under the circumstances the pilot felt the only fair thing to do was to ask his crew how they felt about taking this incredibly dangerous risk. Their helicopter and everyone in it could be blown out of the sky if they took the wounded soldier on board. But if they didn't get him to hospital soon, Channing Moss would almost certainly die from loss of blood.

The four-man crew unanimously agreed that they should try and save their wounded comrade, and so Channing was carefully loaded on board with the RPG in place. As the helicopter lifted off from the battlefield, it was a deadly race against time. Channing needed to be operated on quickly, but it was vital that he was kept as still as possible.

Their helicopter and everyone in it could be blown out of the sky if they took the wounded soldier on board

The Black Hawk headed for an American base called Orgun-E, where an old goat shed had been converted into a small emergency hospital. The medical team there had been told to expect multiple casualties and had been warned that at least one of them was losing a lot of blood. Once again no one said anything about a soldier with a live bomb inside him.

Indeed, when the officer in charge of the hospital first saw Channing's injuries, he wasn't sure whether he needed to call for a surgical team or the bomb-disposal squad.

Channing's heart rate was by now dangerously high and his blood pressure was falling fast. Two army surgeons quickly peeled away the bandages and could see the RPG's fins sticking out of one side of his body and a large bulge on the other, which was the explosive warhead. Neither of them had seen an RPG before but they knew the rules: just as he shouldn't have been allowed on to the helicopter, the wounded private shouldn't have been brought into their hospital either.

Luckily for Channing, it turned out that there was a bomb-disposal expert at Orgun-E. Incredibly, Staff Sergeant Daniel Brown had just been watching a television programme about a patient who arrived at a hospital with a grenade inside him. That story had been fictional but now, unbelievably, something almost identical was happening in real life.

Making his way to the hospital as fast as he could, Daniel couldn't understand why the RPG hadn't gone off. He'd seen plenty of these weapons during his time in the army and couldn't believe Channing was still alive. He knew he was well placed to help the two doctors though, and after reaching the old goat shed he advised everyone who wasn't needed for the operation to get out immediately.

The surgeons, John Oh and Kevin Kirk, were understandably scared by what they were looking at – scared for Channing Moss and scared for themselves. But like Jared and the helicopter crew, they were determined to do something. With help from Daniel, they set out to save Channing's life.

Using an ordinary hacksaw, Daniel carefully removed the finned section of the RPG. It was a good start, but Channing still had live explosives inside his abdomen and he was still in terrible danger from his injuries. At one point his heart actually stopped beating and, while the surgeons struggled to restart it and to keep him alive, it was left to the explosives' expert to slowly ease the front part of the bloodied missile clear of Channing's body.

This was possibly the most dangerous moment so far: the bomb was out but it was still a live bomb. As calmly as he could, Daniel lifted it away from the operating table and slowly carried it out of the room. Being careful not to make any sudden movements, he then walked the bomb out of the building to a spot where it could be safely detonated.

With the RPG out of the way, John and Kevin could now do their best to repair Channing's shattered pelvis and his badly damaged organs. Even by the standards of an army hospital, the soldier's injuries were extraordinarily severe, but against all the odds the surgeons' hard work was successful. It took several operations before he could be moved, and still more of them before Channing Moss could return home to America and to his wife and daughters.

When he did it was in a wheelchair, but Channing Moss was determined to walk again. After months of exercise and painful physiotherapy 'the man with bomb inside him' managed it: Channing was able to stand and to walk when he received a medal, and when he was reunited with the friends and comrades who had saved his life while risking their own.

Channing Moss was determined to walk again

Ian Riches and Stuart Gold
Rescuing the rescuers
(Pacific Ocean, 2005)

The Russian navy's AS-28 is a small underwater craft which was specifically designed to rescue sailors trapped in much larger submarines stuck on the ocean floor.

With a strong titanium metal hull it can operate a thousand metres below the surface, at a depth where the water pressure would crush most machines in a few seconds. The AS-28 can't travel very far under its own power though, and with only a limited supply of oxygen it's not designed to stay submerged for more than a few hours at a time.

In normal use, the AS-28 dives down and is attached to the stricken submarine. The trapped sailors can then climb into the submersible through a special hatch called an airlock. Once they have done this, the AS-28 is quickly piloted back to the surface and the crew transfers on to a waiting boat.

Occasionally something goes wrong, however, and in 2005 the propeller of the AS-28 got tangled up in several undersea cables. At the time the submersible was working about 200 metres beneath the surface, somewhere off the coast of Russia's far-eastern Kamchatka region. The crew of the AS-28 knew it would be impossible for them to swim to the surface from such a depth and sent out a distress signal.

The propeller of the AS-28 got tangled up in several undersea cables

Ordinarily the submersible carried a crew of four, but on this occasion there were seven sailors on board. They had seven compressed air cylinders with them, three and a half litres of drinking water and a couple of packets of crackers. The air would normally be enough to keep them alive for seventy-two hours, but this is far longer than the battery-powered AS-28 was designed to stay underwater. They carefully rationed the water and the biscuits, but it was vital that a rescue bid got under way as soon as possible.

At first the Russians considered using explosives to dislodge the submarine, but this idea was quickly abandoned as too dangerous. Next a pair of powerful tugboats attempted to run their own cables underneath the submarine so they could slowly winch it back to the surface. This didn't work because the cables tangled up in the propeller were attached to a sixty-tonne block of concrete lying on the ocean floor.

Russian submarine crews had died in incidents like this before, including a few years earlier when an on-board explosion crippled the nuclear submarine *Kursk*. That time, everyone on board had been killed, a total of 118 officers and men. Anxious to avoid another tragedy of this sort, the Russians asked for international assistance.

At first the Russians considered using explosives to dislodge the submarine

Britain's Royal Navy, the Japanese Maritime Self-Defense Force, and the US navy all offered their support immediately. Before long several ships were in position above the submersible, and specialist diving teams and equipment began flying thousands of miles to Russia from Britain, Canada and the USA.

Meanwhile, down in the AS-28, the seven crew were doing everything they could to preserve their supplies of oxygen. This meant moving around as little as possible and staying silent, because even talking uses up air. The submarine wasn't particularly cramped (it was designed to rescue twenty sailors at a time) but it was totally dark once the lights were switched off to save power.

It was also bitterly cold. The AS-28's titanium hull wasn't insulated because it wasn't meant to spend very long underwater. Even in summer the water temperature this far down is only a couple of degrees above freezing, so the sailors all huddled together to keep warm. Most of the time they lay side by side on the floor, changing places every now and then so that the men at either end didn't get too cold.

The sailors couldn't hear anything outside the submarine and after a while they began to think that, like their comrades on the much larger *Kursk*, they were being left to die. In reality, up above them, there was plenty going on.

The British team arrived first with a mini-submersible of their own. This was a type known as a submersible craft for ocean repair, position, inspection and observation (SCORPIO). It had been flown more than 4,500 miles from Scotland **The water temperature this far down is only a couple of degrees above freezing** to Kamchatka in a gigantic American military transport plane called a Boeing C-17 Globemaster III. After being unloaded, it was taken out to the AS-28 on board an old Russian ship.

The team in charge of the SCORPIO was under the command of Ian Riches, a Royal Navy officer. He was accompanied by Stuart Gold from a specialist submarine rescue company which uses unmanned vehicles operated by remote control. Both men were experts at this sort of thing, but getting their equipment out to Kamchatka had taken many, many hours. By the time the SCORPIO was in position, the sailors on the AS-28 had been trapped underwater for more than two days.

Unlike the AS-28, the SCORPIO has no room on board for rescuing endangered submariners. Instead Ian and Stuart planned to use its bright lights and cameras to locate the tangle of cables caught up in the Russians' propeller. These could then be sliced through using claws and cutting equipment attached to the ends of the SCORPIO's twin robotic arms.

Unfortunately when it was ready to be lowered into the sea, a final check of the SCORPIO's systems revealed that some of its equipment was

malfunctioning. This meant more time had to be spent dismantling and repairing it before the rescue attempt could begin.

Even working round the clock it took until almost midday on Sunday to fix everything so that Stuart and Ian were able to try another launch. The Russian sailors had been trapped since Thursday afternoon, which meant that sixty-seven of their seventy-two hours of air had already been used up.

Unsurprisingly they were beginning to lose heart. Several of them had written short farewell notes to their families, saying goodbye in the belief that they wouldn't survive. It's not hard to imagine how delighted they must have been when they heard a tapping noise outside the submersible. It was the sound of the SCORPIO's metal claw on the titanium hull. The men were excited, but exhausted from a lack of oxygen. They managed to tap back and hoped that someone would hear them.

It was the sound of the SCORPIO's metal claw on the titanium hull

Ian and Stuart, meanwhile, began to search for the cables using the SCORPIO's remote controls. It didn't take them long to find them, and one after another a total of four steel cables were located, lifted and cut. Each time one was sliced through the AS-28 shifted slightly, but even after all four had been severed it still wasn't free. The cameras showed there was still one more cable to go, but unfortunately, during the process, the AS-28 had collided with the SCORPIO. This had bent its claw so the rescue had to be halted.

Fixing it took another half an hour, by which time the sailors on the AS-28 were beginning to fall ill due to the lack of air. Their seventy-two hours were nearly up when the SCORPIO was sent back down again to sever the final cable with its new claw. Everyone waited nervously, but the AS-28 still wouldn't come up.

Stuart could only think of one possible solution, which was for the dying sailors to attempt a procedure called an emergency ballast tank blow. This forces the water out of the tanks that help a submarine to submerge. It takes only a few seconds and is designed to increase a submarine's buoyancy. Stuart hoped it would enable the AS-28 to float free from whatever was holding it to the seafloor.

Two hundred metres above the trapped men, Russians, Britons, Americans and Japanese all held their breath waiting to see what would happen. Everyone knew the sailors had only minutes left before their air was all gone. The tension was unbearable, but then, as the seconds ticked away, someone spotted a rush of turbulence at the surface. Moments later, the red and white AS-28 bobbed violently to the surface. The ballast tank blow had been successful.

Everyone knew the sailors had only minutes left before their air was all gone

Stuart's lucky, last-ditch trick had worked. The rescuers raced forward to open the submersible's hatches and free the men. The Russian sub was on the surface, but until the hatches were opened the men inside were still at risk from suffocation. In their weakened state the sailors needed help getting out, but they'd been rescued with only seconds to spare.

RESCUE AT ENTEBBE
Commandos storm an airport (Uganda, 1976)

For several years during the 1960s and 1970s airline passengers around the world found themselves at great risk from a new kind of air piracy known as hijacking. During a hijack, terrorists smuggle weapons on to an ordinary plane and then use them to force the pilot to fly to a different destination. After landing, the passengers and crew were usually threatened and held to ransom. Sometimes they were murdered if the terrorists' demands weren't met, and occasionally a captured aircraft was blown up and destroyed.

In June 1976 a French airliner was hijacked during a flight to Paris from Tel Aviv in Israel. The journey included a stopover in Greece, and when the plane landed at Athens four terrorists came on board in disguise. The four hijackers – a German couple and two Arabs – then pulled out guns and grenades, and ordered pilot Michel Bacos to fly them to Libya in North Africa and then on to Uganda.

When the plane landed at Athens four terrorists came on board in disguise

The Ugandan president, Idi Amin, was a supporter of terrorism. He allowed the plane to land at Entebbe (Uganda's main airport) and personally welcomed all four terrorists when they arrived. As well as permitting several more terrorists to join the gang, he gave them additional guns and ammunition. He even brought in his own soldiers to help get the 247 terrified passengers off the plane and into a disused airport terminal.

Inside the building the hostages were separated into two groups. After a couple of days the first group was allowed to go free, but nearly a hundred Jewish and Israeli passengers were kept prisoner. Captain Bacos and his crew bravely decided to stay with them rather than flying home to Paris.

When the gang threatened to kill their hostages, agents working for Mossad, the Israeli secret service, devised a complex rescue plan called Operation Thunderbolt. While negotiations got under way with the terrorists (who wanted $5 million to return the plane) the agents began preparing for one of the most daring long-distance rescue missions ever attempted.

The original idea was to parachute soldiers into Lake Victoria as this is situated very close to the airport. It's the largest lake in the whole of Africa and very beautiful. Unfortunately it is also home to ferocious, man-eating crocodiles. These creatures weigh up to a tonne each and one village on the shoreline, Luganga, has lost more than eighty people in crocodile attacks. The Israelis decided it would be safer to attack the airport directly, and after obtaining permission to fly over Kenya they began selecting pilots and soldiers for the mission.

The new plan involved flying these soldiers and their equipment more than 2,500 miles to Entebbe. This would have to be done in complete secrecy using four Israeli Air Force C-130 Hercules transport aircraft. The rescue party would have to cross several hostile countries to reach Uganda and, for much of the journey, they would be accompanied by two Boeing 707 jets. One of these had been converted into an emergency hospital in case any of the hostages or troops were injured in the assault. The second would oversee the operation.

The aircraft were ordered to stay as low as possible to avoid showing up on enemy radar systems

After taking off from Tel Aviv, the aircraft were ordered to stay as low as possible to avoid showing up on enemy radar systems. For much of the eight-hour flight they flew no more than thirty metres above sea level. The first one reached Entebbe Airport right on schedule, at around 11 p.m., and landed in total darkness.

The element of surprise was vital to the success of this mission. None of the commandos expected any of the terrorists to surrender without a fight and it seemed highly likely that President Amin's soldiers would also try to shoot at them.

As part of Mossad's plan, two Land Rovers and a luxurious black

Mercedes saloon had been loaded on to one of the transport planes before it took off. The first group of commandos used these to drive from the runway to the terminal. They hoped they would be mistaken for Amin and his bodyguards, who usually travelled around Uganda in similar vehicles. If the trick worked, they might be able to enter the terminal without being shot at.

If the trick worked, they might be able to enter the terminal without being shot at

At the same time, another team of commandos leapt out of a second Hercules and set off across the airport. Their job was to destroy a squadron of fighter jets which were parked near the runway. This had to be done to prevent pilots of the Ugandan air force attempting to shoot down the Israeli aircraft when they took off again carrying the freed hostages.

Unfortunately, by the time the first rescue squad reached the airport building, one of the airport guards had realised that something wasn't right. He started shooting at the Israelis, and others joined in. Even so, despite the noise of gunfire, the commandos managed to make it into the terminal quickly enough to surprise the hijackers. When the first terrorist reached for his gun, he was immediately shot. Two more were killed moments later.

The commotion surprised the hostages as well as the terrorists. They didn't know what was going on and many thought they were being attacked until the soldiers explained they had come from Israel to rescue them. Shouting instructions in Hebrew, which only the hostages would be able to understand, the commandos ordered everyone to lie down on the floor. The remaining terrorists were shot and killed in the fighting that followed, along with several of the soldiers Amin had sent in to help them.

When the shooting stopped, the hostages were quickly shepherded out to the waiting aircraft. As soon as they were on board the first one taxied along the runway and took off. The whole operation had taken just fifty minutes.

Tragically, the Israeli commander, Yoni Netanyahu, had been killed in the first few minutes, along with three of the passengers. A fourth, seventy-four-year-old Dora Bloch, was murdered shortly afterwards (on the orders of Amin), but overall Operation Thunderbolt was judged to be an extraordinary success. Not only had the Israeli commandos managed to rescue 102 hostages out of 106, but as an example of decisive action being taken to deal with international terrorism, the Entebbe rescue led to a dramatic fall in the number of hijackings around the world.

The whole operatio had taken just fift minutes

THE WILD BOARS

Trapped in a cave by rising water (Thailand, 2018)

It was early summer when twelve young footballers and their coach disappeared while exploring a complicated network of caves beneath a mountain in northern Thailand. The boys' families and friends were desperate to find them, and television crews from around the world rushed to the Chiang Rai region to report on the search for the missing group.

The caves penetrated deep into the mountain, and for several days no one knew precisely where the boys were or why they hadn't come out. They belonged to a team called the Wild Boars and were aged between eleven and sixteen. The team's exciting jungle adventure was organised by their coach, Ekapol Chantawong, and the alarm had been raised when they failed to return home as planned.

We now know that, once inside the caves, the thirteen had become trapped by the rising waters from Asia's annual monsoon or rainy season.

Coach Ek did what he could to keep the team's morale up while they waited

Coach Ek, as the boys called him, realised they could not escape on their own, and he did what he could to keep the team's morale up while they waited in the cold and pitch black.

Everyone searching for the boys knew they had to be found as quickly as possible. Their emergency supplies were thought to be almost non-existent. The adventure was meant to be a simple day trip into the wilderness, so it was unlikely that anyone in the group was carrying enough food or water to survive for a long period underground.

The heavy rain made their situation even more perilous. In parts of Asia nearly two-and-a-half metres of water can fall in just two days. This is far more than anywhere in Europe sees in an entire year. In northern Thailand, one of the world's wettest regions during the monsoon, it frequently rains for days on end. Widespread flooding is common in towns and cities, and in the countryside the storms can be even more dangerous. With little or no warning, caves like those at Tham Luang quickly fill with rainwater rushing in from above.

Because of this, military divers were brought to the caves, members of the Royal Thai Navy elite SEALs team. Unfortunately, with the network of caves stretching so far underground, it was soon obvious that other, more specialist help was required.

Expert divers Rick Stanton and John Volanthen of the British Cave Rescue Council were called in, and on arriving in the area they began to search the maze of underground passageways and caverns. More support soon arrived from China, Australia and the USA, while the local police brought in sniffer dogs. Drones and robots were also used in the hunt for clues on the surface as to the whereabouts of the boys and their coach.

They began to search the maze of underground passageways

Even with so many people, however, more than a week went by without any good news. Divers searching deep inside the caves found they could make only very slow progress. Visibility under the surface of the water was terrible, and strong currents made their task harder still and even more dangerous. At one point the hunt had to be suspended because of the weather.

Finally, at around 10 p.m. on the ninth day of searching, there was some good news. As Stanton and Volanthen made their way into yet another cavern deep inside the mountain, they poked their heads above the surface of the murky water and were greeted by thirteen smiling, nervous faces.

Sitting on a narrow rock ledge around four kilometres in from the entrance to Tham Luang, the boys and their coach were overjoyed to see their rescuers. Completely exhausted, they were so dazed and confused by their long ordeal that none of them knew what day it was or even how long they had been trapped underground. Rick and John were nevertheless confident that everyone in the group was reasonably healthy – but it was clear that the boys and Ek were still a long way from safety.

The two men explained that members of the SEALs would now be able to supply them with food, water and first aid as well as getting messages out to their anxious parents. But they also said this would take time. The flooding meant that even a professional diver needed at least six hours to reach this far into the cave. Getting out again could take longer still. Even assuming the boys could swim (and several couldn't), none of them had any experience of diving.

Even assuming the boys could swim (and several couldn't), none of them had any experience of diving

As the search operation turned into a rescue mission, an incredible 10,000 people became involved. They included at least 100 divers, 900 policemen and 2,000 soldiers. Thousands of volunteers from dozens of different countries arrived to help. Many were kept busy trying to pump water out from the caves, and navy SEALs took turns underground looking after the boys.

The trouble was, nobody knew quite how to get the boys out. Nine days earlier they had clambered easily into the caves on foot. To get out again they would need to swim and squeeze through several kilometres of flooded passages while wearing breathing apparatus. Even if such an operation was possible it would be incredibly dangerous, something soon demonstrated by the tragic death of former SEAL Saman Gunan, whose oxygen ran out in one of the flooded tunnels.

One suggestion was to drill an escape shaft down from above, but this was quickly ruled out. Drilling down through hundreds of metres of mountain would take far too long, and there was a risk that the boys would be injured

or even killed if any rocks were dislodged during the mining operation. Next it was suggested that Ek and the team stay in the cave until the end of the monsoon season. Divers could take in all the food and bedding they needed to be reasonably comfortable, and eventually they would be able to crawl out just as they had clambered in. But this would mean the boys staying down in the dark for many weeks or even months. The whole idea sounded terrifying, and in the end this plan was also abandoned.

It turned out that, even with the many noisy pumps operating above, the floodwater was threatening to rise even higher than the rocky ledge inside the cave. If this happened, the rescuers knew there was a very real risk the boys would run out of air.

The increased danger meant that the only practical solution was to bring the team out as quickly as possible. An American billionaire offered to provide a miniature submarine for the task, but it was felt that even the smallest submersible would get stuck in the twisted, narrow rock passageways and block their exit. Instead the boys would have to put on masks and oxygen tanks and then be pushed and pulled through the flooded tunnels by the most expert divers on the rescue team.

The only practical solution was to bring the team out as quickly as possible

This sort of rescue had never been attempted before. While the boys were given easy-to-digest, high-energy food to build up their stamina, the divers practised with some Thai schoolchildren in a nearby swimming pool. Each child put on a full-face mask and had an oxygen tank strapped to his chest. Holding on firmly to the children, the divers could then guide them through the water and out to safety.

In the clean, clear water of the swimming pool this plan worked perfectly, but the tunnels were obviously going to be far more challenging. The divers decided they should take the additional precaution of clipping a safety line to each boy. This would prevent anyone drifting away in the murky floodwater, but the operation would still require great skill on the part of the divers and immense courage from the boys. If anyone panicked it could endanger everyone involved.

By the time the rescuers felt ready to put their plan into operation, the young members of the Wild Boars had been trapped underground for an astonishing sixteen days. Everyone was desperate to get them out, but for safety reasons it was decided to bring them out a few at a time. Each trip through the tunnel would take several hours and attempting to do it any faster would just put lives at risk.

The first boy emerged just before six in the evening, and by 8 p.m. another three were out in the fresh air. It was desperately hard work for the divers and the operation was halted overnight to give them a chance to recover while their air tanks were refilled.

Work resumed the following morning, and after several more challenging hours the good news was finally announced to waiting journalists: after seventeen days the lost boys and their coach were out of the cave, and everyone was safe. For the rescuers it was a bittersweet moment. Saman Gunan had died trying to save children he had never even met. His sad death cast a long shadow, but international cooperation, careful planning and many examples of personal heroism had succeeded in saving thirteen young lives.

EPILOGUE

How far would you go to save a life? There is no doubt that the men, women and children in these stories risked their own lives to go to the rescue of other people in danger. Some got involved because they have special skills or training, but others are ordinary people who acted on instinct, when there was no time to delay. Their strength of character and their bravery made all the difference between life and death.

None of the rescuers consider themselves to be anything special, but the people whose lives they saved would disagree. These amazing true stories prove that you don't need superpowers or a mask and cape to be a real-life hero.

DON'T MISS THESE OTHER

WHEN IT COMES TO EXTREME STORIES OF SURVIVAL, FEW CAN MATCH THESE TRUE TALES OF HEROISM

Ranging from classics such as Shackleton's expedition to the Antarctic, to more modern exploits, including the adventurer who inspired the movie *127 Hours*, these courageous survivors all have one thing in common: an incredible ability to draw on all their strength, bravery and self-belief in order to beat the odds, and live to tell their tales ...

INSPIRING COLLECTIONS ...

FOR AS LONG AS THERE HAVE BEEN WARS, ANIMALS HAVE BEEN OUT THERE SAVING LIVES.

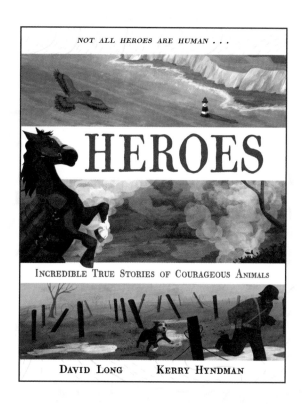

NOT ALL HEROES ARE HUMAN . . .

HEROES

INCREDIBLE TRUE STORIES OF COURAGEOUS ANIMALS

DAVID LONG   KERRY HYNDMAN

Cats, dogs, horses, birds, and even a bear, have shown incredible courage and devotion when going to war alongside mankind, and this book tells their extraordinary stories.